BOXING SHORTS

GRAEME KENT

Illustrations by David Arthur

GUINNESS PUBLISHING

Designed by Kathleen Aldridge

Illustrations by David Arthur

Cover illustration by Robert Heesom

Typeset in Palatino by Ace Filmsetting Ltd, Frome, Somerset

Printed and bound in Great Britain by The Bath Press, Bath

'Guinness' is a registered trademark of Guinness Publishing Ltd

A catalogue record for this book is available from the British Library

ISBN 0–85112–572–7

The author referees the final of the
Solomon Islands middleweight championships

GRAEME KENT's amateur boxing career began much as it was to continue when, in his very first bout, due to an administrative error he found himself fighting the flyweight champion of Great Britain. The next low point occurred on a troop-ship bound for Korea, when he became probably the first private in the British Army ever to have been outpointed by an officer, which meant that he had to spend the rest of the six-week voyage hiding from his fellow other-ranks. A few years later, in the London University championships, in one of the few bouts he actually seemed to be winning, he hit his opponent so hard that he broke his wrist and had to retire.

It was with some relief, after 80 contests, that he abandoned competitive boxing to spend the next 30 years writing about and broadcasting on the sport.

As a BBC producer he directed a radio feature on the life of John Gully, the bare-knuckle fighter who became a Member of Parliament, and wrote a 90-minute *Saturday Night Theatre* play based on the notorious Dempsey–Gibbons fight at Shelby, Montana. He then lived for eight years in the Solomon Islands, where he helped organise the first boxing championships and provided a live radio commentary in pidgin on the bouts. He has written several novels with a boxing background, and among the 60 non-fiction books he has had published are *Fighting Sports*, *Boxing's Strangest Fights* and *A Pictorial History of Wrestling*. He is now the headteacher of a Lincolnshire primary school.

CONTENTS

NOBODY KNOWS THE
TROUBLE I'VE SEEN . . .

British middleweight Jock McAvoy demolished world champion Babe Risko in one round at Madison Square Garden in 1935. Unfortunately the match was made over the middleweight limit, so McAvoy could not make a claim for the title. Risko's connections stalled so long in giving McAvoy a return fight that the Briton lost interest and returned home. He outgrew the middleweight limit and so could not mount another challenge for the championship.

The organisers of the World Amateur Boxing Championships in Sydney, Australia did not have an enviable time. When Cuban featherweight Arnaldo Mesa lost on points to a Korean and then heard that a team-mate had also lost, he went berserk, tried to attack the referee and threw a chair over a partition in the dressing room. Meanwhile, the Yugoslav team trainer was suspended for attacking and threatening the life of a New Zealand referee, and the captain of the Chinese team went into hiding, refused to return to China and asked for political asylum.

Floyd Patterson was so unsure of his chances of regaining his world heavyweight title from Sonny Liston in Las Vegas in 1963 that he took a false beard with him to the stadium, so that if the worst came to the worst he could escape undetected from the arena. Patterson lost in the first round – as he had in his first bout with Liston.

Dimitri Michael had a disagreement with his second after the first round of his contest with Kid Lewis in Australia in 1968. The second took umbrage and stalked out of the hall, taking the stool with him. That meant that the bewildered Michael had to stand on his own in his corner between rounds. An equally confused referee declared the bout to be 'No Contest'.

World heavyweight champion Tommy Burns agreed to let his novice opponent last a few rounds against him in their Paris bout in 1908 when he was matched with Jewey Smith. This way he reckoned that the promoter Leon See and the spectators would get their money's worth. Unfortunately, early in the fight a flash from a camera set fire to some decorations on a wall. The blaze began to spread. Forgetting his agreement, the terrified Burns stunned Smith with one hard blow and turned and raced out of the arena.

Charley Hopkins had to retire in the second round against Fred Guerro in Miami in 1952. He had such a severe case of sunburn that he could not continue.

'Have your passport ready, Mr Robinson'

When Ray Robinson fought Gerhard Hecht in Berlin in 1951 the American was disqualified in the second round for an alleged kidney punch. Enraged Germans stormed the ring and Robinson had to take refuge beneath the roped square until police could escort him from the arena. The referee later changed his verdict to 'No decision', enraging the Germans even more. Robinson and his entourage had to be escorted out of Berlin by American military policemen.

A certain amount of confusion surrounded the world welterweight championship at the turn of the century. In 1904, the Dixie Kid won the title when

'That could be the spark this fight needs!'

Joe Walcott was disqualified for hitting him low. In the row that followed Walcott's manager punched the referee in the mouth. The Dixie Kid did not profit from his title because the following year he went to prison for three years. Walcott claimed the title back but incapacitated himself by shooting himself through the chest while demonstrating the workings of a pistol to a friend.

Many optimistic press agents have claimed that a forthcoming bout 'will set the ring on fire'. This actually happened in 1957 when the Italian deaf-mute Mario D'Agata defended his world bantamweight title against Alphonse Halimi of France in Paris. In the third round the lights over the ring exploded and burst into flame, showering the ring with blazing debris. D'Agata sustained burns to his shoulder, but insisted on fighting on once the ring had been cleared. He lost on points over 12 rounds.

Coming out for the last round of his world light-welterweight title bout against Greg Haugen, Hector Camacho, 'the Macho Man', was even on points. Haugen refused to shake hands before the start of the round, so the incensed Camacho threw a punch at his opponent. The referee promptly docked him a point for fighting before the bell. Camacho lost on a split decision, only to see Haugen stripped of his title after he had tested positive for drugs.

In an international contest held in America in 1866 between Jem Mace of England and Joe Goss of the USA, neither man struck a blow throughout the entire contest. The bored referee stopped the so-called fight and declared it a draw.

Panama Al Brown was given a split decision against local favourite Kid Francis in Marseilles in 1932. A riot broke out. Police managed to smuggle Brown, still in his boxing gear, out to the pier and into a motor boat. He never bothered to go back to claim his pay for the contest.

'Almost there, Monsieur Brown . . .'

Harry Greb and Kid Norfolk, prominent middle and light-heavyweights in the period before World War II, each lost the sight of an eye through being gouged by an opponent.

When heavyweights Joe Jeannette and Sam McVey met in Paris, Jeannette was floored 27 times while McVey went down on 11 occasions before Jeannette won in the 49th round.

After former world welterweight and middleweight champion Micky Walker had defeated Paul Berlenbach in Chicago in 1927, he took on most of the members of the Notre Dame football team. Walker was staying at the same hotel as the football players, who had just lost to the Army 18–0. The disgruntled footballers picked a fight with Walker's diminutive but fiery manager Doc Kearns. Walker tried to pacify the students but was compelled to knock eight of them out before the others saw reason.

At the Newark Armoury in 1920, Al Roberts of Staten Island was on the verge of pulling off an enormous upset when he landed a crude but effective right-hand to the jaw of promising young light-heavyweight Gene Tunney. Tunney's knees buckled and Roberts moved in for the kill, as his supporters in the crowd cheered and blew horns.

Unfortunately one of them also rang a bell. Roberts assumed that this signified the end of the round. Obediently he turned and trotted back to his corner. By the time his frantic seconds had persuaded him that the round

was still in progress, Tunney's head was clear. The ex-Marine proceeded to outbox his opponent and stop him in seven rounds. Roberts was never heard of again. Gene Tunney became heavyweight champion of the world six years later.

Joe Walcott, welterweight champion of the world 1896–1906, disappeared in 1935. Together with a group of friends he had been on his way to Hollywood, hoping to pick up some work there. They broke the journey overnight at Mansfield, Ohio. Walcott left the hotel to pick up some medicine for one of his friends and never returned.

World heavyweight champion James Braddock was living on state benefit before he won the title. When asked what his success was due to, he replied, 'Opening the door and finding no milk on the step!'

Manager Doc Kearns guided heavyweight Jack Dempsey from obscurity to the world title. After the two men fell out because Dempsey objected to Kearns taking 50% of everything he earned, Kearns pursued his former protegé with a hail of writs. Dempsey was hounded by process-servers slapping writs on him, his bank accounts were sealed off and he became ill through worry.

Light-heavyweight King Levinsky was managed by his

sister Lena. His big chance came when he was matched in an exhibition bout with heavyweight champion Max Baer. Lena told her brother to show Baer up, meaning that the skilful Levinsky should outbox the bigger man. Levinsky thought that Lena wanted him to attempt to outslug the hard-hitting champion. Dutifully he went in swinging against Baer, and was knocked flat in two rounds.

While Bill Neat was training for the unsuccessful defence of his bare-knuckle championship against Tom Spring in 1823, he was visited by two Quaker ladies who tried to persuade him to abandon the ring. Afterwards, the shaken Neat said with feeling that he would rather have faced Spring for two hours than either of those ladies for half the time and double the money.

In 1956 everything began to go wrong for promising young British heavyweight Henry Cooper. After having the better of Peter Bates for most of their contest he sustained a cut eye and retired in the fifth round of the Manchester bout. Cooper's next fight was for the British Empire title in February 1957, when he was knocked out in nine rounds by Joe Bygraves. Three months later Cooper went to Stockholm and was knocked out in five rounds by Ingemar Johansson for the European championship. In September of 1957 Cooper lost over 15 rounds to Joe Erskine for the British heavyweight title.

There was a false dawn when he outpointed Hans Kalbfell in Dortmund, but in January 1958 he could only draw with Heinz

Neuhaus, also in Dortmund. Three months later Cooper was disqualified in the fourth round against another German opponent, Erich Schoeppner, in Frankfurt. Next Cooper was matched against the dangerous Welsh heavyweight Dick Richardson at Porthcawl. It must have seemed like the end of the road for Cooper when he was floored in the fifth round, but gamely he got to his feet. Richardson rushed wildly at him and Cooper knocked him out with one punch. It was the turning point. Cooper went on to defeat Joe Erskine for the British and Empire heavyweight titles and later to win the European championship.

Richardson pulled off the best victory of his career when he took the European heavyweight championship from Hans Kalbfell in a bout in Dortmund in 1960. Richardson was so much on top that the referee stopped the bout in the 13th round. Richardson did not understand that the fight was over and brought over another right hand. As Kalbfell had dropped his hands, the crowd went wild, demanding that the Welsh fighter be disqualified. The referee replied that he had already stopped the bout, so he could do nothing about what happened afterwards.

The owner of a 'Try Your Strength' machine to test the power of a man's punch blenched when he saw the enormous William Perry, 'the Tipton Slasher', approach his machine, on display at a Handsworth race meeting in 1851. He begged the

prize-fighter not to chance his arm. It was in vain. Perry threw one punch at the mark and the whole apparatus disintegrated. The sporting crowd took up a collection to reimburse the stricken showman.

In their bout at Mar Del Plata in Argentina, Antonio Cuevas knocked his opponent Lala Landini through the ropes and into the ringside seats. Landini

sat calmly in one of the seats while he was counted out, refusing the entreaties of his seconds to get back into the ring.

Joe Bugner put an end to the careers of two men who had held the British heavyweight title. In 1970 he defeated Brian London in five rounds, and a year later he outpointed Henry Cooper. Neither of the losers fought again.

'Title? What title? It's comfortable here'

A stormy contest

The Chick Calderwood–Piero Del Papa European light-heavyweight contest held in Liagnano, Italy in 1966 took place in a terrible storm in an open-air arena. There were great flashes of lightning and the ring lamps exploded. In the sixth round, with the fighters skidding all over the soaked ring, the referee called the bout off and declared it 'No contest'.

Heavyweight champion Joe Louis and future world welterweight and middleweight champion Sugar Ray Robinson both served in the segregated US Army in World War II. On one occasion they were ordered out of a bus waiting-room reserved for whites. Louis moved without complaint but Robinson swung a punch at one of the military policemen moving them on.

When an English amateur team met a team of Welsh internationals, both Henry Cooper and Joe Bygraves were in the English team. Each was disqualified by the same referee. Back in the dressing room an enraged Bygraves knocked the referee out. He was banned for life from amateur boxing and turned professional. As Henry Cooper pointed out, he didn't have much choice.

Many people thought that challenger Jersey Joe Walcott had outpointed Joe Louis in their first fight for the world heavyweight championship in New York in 1947. Louis seemed to think so as well, because he tried to leave the ring before the result was announced and had to be restrained by his seconds, but he was declared the winner.

Marty Servo might just as well not have bothered to win the world welterweight championship. When he took the title from Freddie Cochrane in 1946, he had to guarantee the champion so much money that he actually had to pay $8000 out of his own pocket. Before he could cash in on the title Servo was knocked out in two rounds by middleweight Rocky Graziano. In the process Servo's nose was damaged so badly that he was forced to retire from the ring and never got around to defending his costly welterweight title.

Heavyweights Riddick Bowe and Elijah Carl Tillery continued fighting after the bell in Washington in 1991. Tillery then kicked Bowe. Bowe's manager jumped up onto the apron of the ring, seized Tillery round the neck from behind, hauled him over the top rope and dropped him onto the floor of the hall. Tillery was disqualified and a riot broke out.

TRICKS OF THE TRADE

Even the most superlative boxers have their off-days. Kid McCoy was one of the most skilful boxers ever to enter the ring, yet when he met unknown Jack McCormick in Chicago in 1899 he walked into a sucker punch and was knocked out in the first round. Where McCormick made his mistake was in granting the Kid a return bout. They met again in New York a few months later and McCoy gave his opponent one of the most dreadful thrashings ever seen in a ring. He could easily have knocked McCormick out, but each time he had the other man dazed on the ropes he would step back and allow him to recover, so that he could resume handing out punishment. McCoy won on points over eight rounds.

Spike Robson, an English lightweight and featherweight, was a boxer who liked to keep up a stream of verbal abuse against his opponents. When he fought Jim Driscoll at the National Sporting Club in London in 1910 he closed both of Driscoll's eyes, so the British featherweight champion could see nothing. However, Robson kept up his running commentary to such a degree that in the 15th round Driscoll tracked his opponent down by his voice alone and threw over a knock-out punch, silencing Robson at last.

American welterweight Willie Lewis was a great favourite in France before World War I. While training in a Paris gymnasium he taught his favourite deadly 'one-two' combination of punches to a young French boxer working out in the same gymnasium. A few years later, in 1912, Lewis fought the young Frenchman in earnest in a Paris hall. Georges Carpentier won handily over 20 rounds, mainly through his effective use of the 'one-two' punches.

World featherweight champion Terrible Terry McGovern was scheduled to defend his title against an unknown called Young Corbett at Hartford, Connecticut in 1901. Everyone expected McGovern to win easily. En route to the ring Corbett banged on the door of McGovern's dressing room, and yelled, 'Come out, you bum, and take your beating!' When the bout started, the enraged McGovern lost his cool and tore into Corbett. Corbett boxed rings round the wild champion and knocked him out in the second round.

Whenever possible Harry Greb, world middleweight champion, would make love to a girl in his dressing room before a contest.

When black heavyweight Sam Langford was matched against the fearsome Fred Fulton in Boston in 1917, he asked his friend and sometimes opponent Harry Wills the best way to defeat the white fighter. 'The best way,' advised Wills judiciously, 'is to take a club and hit him on

Come on, he's not THAT good!'

the head with it. Then, when he turns round, hit him with that club again. One thing, though. If you miss with that second shot you'd better start running, else you're dead!'

When dazzling boxer Jim Driscoll toured with Harry Culliss' boxing booth at the beginning of the 20th century, times in the Midlands were hard. No challengers could be found to try their luck with the magnificent featherweight. In desperation Culliss offered a guinea to anyone in the crowd who could manage to land one punch on the Welshman.

Joseph Corrara adopted the ring name of Johnny Dundee, and so was known as 'the Scotch Wop'. He developed a technique of gathering momentum by bouncing off the ropes and launching a fierce attack at an opponent. Against Willy Jackson in 1917 Dundee mistimed the move. He bounced straight into Jackson's right hand and was knocked out in the first round.

Spike Robson thought he had worked out the perfect defence against the potent right hand of American Joe Gans in their 1908 Philadelphia bout. The cagey English fighter fought behind a raised left shoulder, with his right hand held defensively across his jaw. Such a tight defence gave Gans no chance of a clear shot at Robson's chin. But Gans did not need one. Instead he smashed his lethal right against Robson's protective glove. The force of the blow smashed the Englishman's fist against his own jaw and knocked him clear out of the ring.

Sam Russell was the referee when featherweights Johnny Curley and Joe Fox met at Brighton during Race Week. In the first round a wild swing from one of the fighters dislodged the

Robson's defence is well and truly spiked . . .

spectacles from Russell's nose and shattered them. The fight was held up while Russell tried on the glasses of ringsiders, until he found a pair which improved his sight. The bout went on but ended in a riot, with the referee hiding under the ring and announcing his decision there!

Light-heavyweight Jack Delaney knocked out his opponent Tiger Flowers in the second round of their 1925 New York bout. Flowers' manager claimed that his fighter had beaten the count, and as the crowd was looking ugly, Delaney reluctantly agreed to fight on. Two rounds later he

'These would look good on you'

18

hit Flowers so hard that the fighter was unconscious for several minutes. When he came round, Flowers sought out Delaney and said, 'I'd like to tell you that I'm convinced!'

Before his bout with Jim Maloney in 1927, Delaney broke training and went on a drinking spree. In the course of the evening he got into a dispute with a porter on a railway train. The drunken Delaney threw a punch at the porter, who ducked. Delaney broke his right hand on the steel side of the train. He told no one of his trouble and did not throw his right hand once in the bout. Maloney won on points and Delaney's career petered out.

Just before the outbreak of World War I, Irish heavyweight Nutty Curran went to Paris to fight Kid McCoy, one of the great all-round tricksters, though he was almost 40 years old by this time. In the 12th round Curran floored McCoy. The American crawled over to the apron of the ring, where a spectator had placed his brandy and soda. McCoy drained the glass and got up, much refreshed, to outpoint his opponent.

When American Willie Ritchie won the world lightweight title in 1912 he soon discovered that making the weight limit of 133 lbs was very difficult. Scorning traditional weight-reducing methods, Ritchie merely declared that the lightweight limit was now 135 lbs.

Ring experts began to suspect that heavyweight champion Jack Dempsey was past his best when two lighter men showed up well against him in training bouts. Middleweight Harry Greb gave the champion such a torrid time that he promptly challenged the heavyweight to a title match, but was rejected because he was 'too small'. Light-heavyweight Tommy Loughran completely outboxed Dempsey in their training sessions. A number of onlookers placed substantial bets on Gene Tunney to dethrone Dempsey, and this duly happened at Philadelphia in 1926, Tunney winning on points.

Boxing is noted for its 'opponents', fighters imported to give local favourites easy victories, thus sending the patrons home happy. In the 1940s, one such group of no-hopers toured the USA, making up the losing halves of boxing bills, guaranteed not to trouble the home-town fighters. This original troupe was named after its city of origin, being known as the Philadelphia Death Squad.

Fifty years later there were protests about the quality of certain American and Mexican boxers imported into Britain to boost the records of local fighters. Many of them hit the canvas so quickly that they were given the collective title of the Tijuana Tumblers. Disgruntled British middleweight Nigel Benn complained that he was disgusted with being fed a diet of Mexican road sweepers.

Fritzie Zivic was regarded as being an expert at boxing's less noble side. He was adept with the head, the thumb and the punch below the belt. His great ambition was to earn enough in the ring to be able to afford a Cadillac and when he was matched with Henry Armstrong for the world welterweight title in 1940, he thought that his chance had come. The problem was that he knew he could never beat the gifted Armstrong in a clean fight. In the bout, Armstrong outsmarted Zivic for the first eight rounds. 'I saw that Cadillac going farther and farther away,' recalled Zivic later. In the ninth round Armstrong at last responded to Zivic's dirty tricks with a few foul tactics of his own. The referee shrugged. 'If you two want to fight that way it's all right with me,' he grunted. 'That,' said Zivic happily, 'was when I saw that Cadillac turn right round and come driving back towards me!' Zivic won a rough bout on points.

Barbados light-heavyweight champion Kid Ralph was far too good for his opponent Kid Francis in their 1951 contest, knocking him out in the eighth round. Before he could leave the ring, supporters of Francis poured in. They intimidated the referee and forced both boxers to carry on fighting. Ralph won on points over ten rounds.

Lee Oma did not prepare well for his fight against British champion Bruce Woodcock in London in 1948. For his part Woodcock had recently been badly beaten by the American Joe Baksi and was extremely apprehensive about making any attacks. Between rounds Oma gasped to his seconds, 'If this guy doesn't knock me down soon I'm going to fall down!' Eventually Woodcock landed a semblance of a punch and Oma crumpled unconvincingly to the canvas, where he remained while the enraged crowd sang 'Lay down, lay down,' to the tune of 'Bow Bells'.

When Muhammad Ali made his bid to regain the world heavyweight title by challenging George Foreman in Kinshasa, Zaire in 1974, everyone expected the former champion to box at long distance against the gigantic and heavy-hitting Foreman. Instead Ali spent most of the contest leaning on the ropes, allowing Foreman to punch himself into a state of exhaustion. When the challenger judged the champion to have punched himself out, Ali moved in and knocked Foreman out in the eighth round. Ali later referred to this technique as 'rope-a-dope'.

In his autobiography *Minter*, former world middleweight champion Alan Minter tells of his contest against Maurice Thomas in London in 1972. Thomas and his manager had travelled down from Bradford. The boxer came in overweight and was given an hour in which to get rid of the excess poundage. The Northerner and his manager went out in search of a sauna. Unfortunately, being strangers to the capital, they were unaware that in central London 'sauna' was usually a euphemism for a rather more dubious establishment. The two bewildered men hurried from topless parlour to topless parlour, unable to find an ordinary steam bath. When they returned to the stadium Thomas was still overweight.

'That wasn't quite what I had
in mind, Miss'

Lightweight champion Benny Leonard was noted for his impeccable ring appearance, with his slicked-back glossy hair. When he fought Leo Johnson in New York in 1917, Johnson's handlers told their man to rush out at the opening bell and ruffle Leonard's hair, thus making the champion lose his cool. The first part of the plan worked. In accordance with the game plan Johnson bounced across the ring at the first bell and cuffed Leonard's neatly arranged hair-style. The second part of the plan worked also, but only up to a point. Leonard did lose his temper, but to such an extent that he stormed into Johnson and knocked him out in the first round.

Michael Spinks was an excellent world light-heavyweight champion, but everyone thought that he would be far too light to pose any problems for massive Larry Holmes when he challenged for the world heavyweight title in 1985 at Las Vegas. Spinks amazed everyone by increasing his weight from 175 lbs to 204 lbs, without losing any of his speed, and gaining a narrow points decision.

One of the noisiest preambles to a contest must have taken place at Leicester in 1951 when Terry Allen successfully defended his

The hair is Leonard's achilles heel

22

This fight's in the bag . . .

British flyweight championship against Vic Herman of Scotland. Herman's gimmick was to enter the ring playing the bagpipes. Not to be outdone Allen insisted on being escorted by a piano-accordionist playing a selection of Cockney songs.

Future world heavyweight champion James J Corbett had hardly started out on his boxing career when he found himself stranded and penniless in Salt Lake City, after he and a friend had eloped with two young ladies and married them. Corbett saw an advertisement in a newspaper from a professional fighter called Frank Smith, challenging any man in Utah to a bout. Corbett was in no condition to fight, but it was that or starvation, so accordingly he challenged Smith.

Corbett was so outwardly confident and always dressed so well that Smith believed that his challenger was really the British champion Charlie Mitchell, trying to pick up some easy money under an alias. Corbett was only too pleased to foster the deception and graciously agreed not to hit Smith too hard when they met. He persuaded Smith to take a dive before he got hurt by 'Mitchell'. When the fight started Corbett tried to give a convincing impression of Charlie Mitchell's style and Smith went down from a light tap, to the considerable relief of the exhausted Corbett.

American lightweight Harry Stone would try to gain a psychological advantage over his opponent by entering the ring smoking a cigar. He would hand the lighted cigar to his second, saying loudly that he would be back to finish it in a couple of minutes.

Anything went in the ring in the early days of gloved boxing. On one occasion heavyweight Sam Langford was matched with John Lester Johnson in New York in 1913. Johnson realised that he had no chance against the formidable Langford and ran quickly backwards around the perimeter of the ring. Langford watched his opponent go round several times, then cocked his right hand and waited for his adversary to come by for the third time. As Johnson came within distance Langford let fly at his disappearing form. The

'This won't take long'

24

Tommy's hair is no tonic for Carnera

blow caught Johnson in the small of the back, sending him flat on his face. The big man lay unable to move, his legs paralysed, as the referee counted him out.

When the skilful Tommy Loughran challenged Primo Carnera for the world heavyweight title in Miami in 1934, Loughran scaled 184 lbs to the Italian's 270 lbs. In an effort to dissuade the gigantic champion from mauling him about in the clinches, Loughran smeared his hair with the cheapest and most evil-smelling hair tonic that he could find, and kept thrusting his head under Carnera's nose. Despite his obvious repugnance Carnera still outpointed his smaller opponent.

The manager of Gerardo Martinez protested that his fighter had lost his 1991 world bantamweight contest with champion Raul Perez because someone had sneaked into Martinez's hotel room and greased the soles of his boxing boots, making it impossible for the boxer to gain a secure footing. A laboratory report confirmed

Oiling the wheels, or rather the soles

GERARDO MARTINEZ

SUPE GREAS

that a foreign substance probably had been smeared over the soles of the footwear.

When James J Corbett travelled by train to New Orleans for his successful bid for John L Sullivan's heavyweight title in 1892, he had a gymnasium installed in the baggage car so that he could train right up to the last minute.

In 1800 Jem Belcher defeated Andrew Gamble in ten minutes for the championship of England. Gamble was suspected of 'taking a dive', and a reward of £500 was posted for anyone who could give evidence about this. No one came forward.

Tommy Loughran would train on his own in a gymnasium using an egg-timer which ran out of sand at 2 minutes 50 seconds, to time his rounds. After years of practice Loughran always knew when there were only ten seconds of a round remaining. In a contest he would then retreat to his own corner, so that all he had to do was sit down on his stool when the bell went, while his opponent had to make the long trek back across the ring.

Several boxers have won titles without ever fighting outside their home town. John Kelly took the British and European bantamweight titles from Peter Keenan in 1953. The fight took place in Belfast, as had all of Kelly's previous bouts. Vic Toweel of South Africa won the world featherweight title without ever boxing outside Johannesburg.

When future world light-heavyweight champion Freddie Mills was boxing exhibitions in India while serving in the RAF in World War II, he was most impressed by a young man serving in the West African Armed Forces. The young boxer's name was Roy Ankrah. Mills invited him to return to Britain with him. Ankrah turned down the offer but later made his own way to Scotland to embark upon a professional career which led to his winning the British Empire featherweight title before he returned to become National Boxing Coach for Ghana.

World flyweight champion Jimmy Wilde weighed only about 6½ stone and gained universal admiration when he consistently defeated much bigger opponents. Followers of the game pointed out that although he often gave away more than a stone in weight, Wilde still insisted on many of his opponents reducing to a weight at which they were not strong before he fought them.

Willie Lewis was almost as adept with his tongue as he was with his fists, and made a speciality of worrying his opponents before they entered the ring with him. He was matched against Jewey Smith in Paris in 1909. Smith did not know Lewis, so just before their bout the American entered Smith's dressing-room clad in full evening dress, complete with opera hat. He commiserated with Smith, telling him that he was up against a very good fighter that night. After Lewis had gone out Smith asked his manager who the toff was. 'That's the man you're going to fight tonight,' said his mentor grimly. Lewis won in ten rounds.

On another occasion, Lewis entered the dressing room of Pat O'Keefe just before their 1907 bout in New York. He patted the other fighter's stomach and said, 'You're a great fighter, Pat, but you must be out of your mind going into the ring with a stomach like that on you.' When the bell rang, O'Keefe automatically lowered his guard to protect his body, expecting an onslaught upon it. Instead Lewis knocked him out in the first round with a right to the chin.

As a young man, future world lightweight champion Freddie Welsh talked himself into a job as trainer at an American athletic club. To his dismay a set of new-fangled punchballs were delivered to the club. The members looked on expectantly, waiting for Welsh to display his skills. The problem was that Welsh had never seen a modern punchball. The quick-thinking Welsh hit one of the balls and turned to the salesman. 'These are no good at all,' he said contemptuously. 'The club needs better ones than these!' By the time the new set had been delivered, Welsh had learned how to use them.

Bare-knuckle fighter Joe Ward's training and dietary requirements when preparing for a contest were simple, if drastic: 'Three doses of salts, three sweats, three vomits, three times weekly with victuals three-parts dressed.'

An unexpected prize came the way of Moroccan-born, Manchester-based boxer Najib Daho in 1990 when he took the Commonwealth lightweight title from Pat Doherty. The King of Morocco heard about this success and ordered his ambassador in England to arrange a trip home for the boxer.

In a light-heavyweight bout at Battersea Town Hall in 1990, Lou Gent struck his opponent Cyril Minnius in the body in the third round. Minnius fell to the floor, claiming that he had been fouled. Instead the referee disqualified him for 'feigning injury'.

Infighting – fighting at such close quarters that no proper punches can be thrown – was banned in amateur contests at the beginning of the 20th century. Any amateur attempting to get inside would be stopped by the referee and ordered, 'Box, not fight!'

To prove a point, world featherweight champion Willie Pep once won a round against

Jackie Graves without delivering a punch. The bout took place at Minneapolis in 1946. Pep feinted, ducked and charged, giving such an impression of action that he fooled all the judges, who awarded him the points for the round.

Lee Oma had little chance of defeating Ezzard Charles for the latter's world heavyweight title in 1951. In a forlorn hope of winning on a disqualification, his seconds pulled his shorts up well above the waist-line and noisily claimed that Charles was hitting low every time the champion struck Oma in the body. Finally the experienced referee Ruby Goldstein strode over to Oma's corner and snarled, 'Pull his trunks down before they choke your guy!'

When Muhammad Ali was stripped of his heavyweight title for refusing to be inducted into the US Army, the boxing authorities selected eight heavyweights to compete in a tournament to decide the new champion. They were Joe Frazier, Jerry Quarry, Floyd Patterson, Jimmy Ellis, Karl Mildenberger, Oscar Bonavena, Ernie Terrell

Oma's trunk trick

and Thad Spencer. Frazier refused to take part in the competition. The other heavyweights set out on a laborious series of eliminating bouts, ending with Jimmy Ellis outpointing Jerry Quarry at Oakland in 1968. Then Frazier stepped forward, challenged Ellis and stopped him in five rounds in New York in 1970.

American television tried something new when Ali fought Earnie Shavers in New York in 1977. The judges relayed their scores to the producer, who flashed them on the screen at the end of each round. Ali's shrewd manager Angelo Dundee had a television set installed in the champion's dressing-room and a man sitting before it. The viewer would signal to Dundee whether Ali had won or lost the previous round and the handler would alter the fighter's strategy accordingly. The system of announcing the scores after each round was soon abandoned.

When promoter Jeff Dickson was promoting in Paris at the Palais de Sports between the two world wars, he had a heavy meshed net suspended over the ring. If the spectators started throwing objects at the fighters, he would have the net lowered. The combatants could fight on, but the audience could not see very much.

As a young boxer Jack Johnson was beaten by veteran Joe Choynski. Both men were arrested and sentenced to 24 days in jail for taking part in an illegal prize-fight. To while away the time, the two men sparred behind bars. Choynski gave the younger man a thorough grounding in the fistic arts, which stood him in good stead. Johnson went on to win the world heavyweight title some years later.

MONEY, MONEY, MONEY!

In 1789, bare-knuckle fighter Tom Johnson earned more than £35000 by defeating Isaac Perrins in 62 rounds at Banbury. This total was made up of £10000 which he earned by betting on himself; a gift of £2500 from a gambler called Bullock who had won £25000 on the fight; a gate donation of £3500; and another £20000 from other gamblers who had done well out of the result. Within a year Johnson had gambled all his winnings away. He died in poverty.

One of the toughest of bare-knuckle fighters was John Smith, who fought under the ring name of Buckhorse. When times were hard, as they often were, he would let anyone hit him and knock him down for a few pennies.

John L Sullivan won over $1 million during his career. Only $120000 of this came from his ring earnings. His largest purse was $14000 for fighting Herbert Slade in 1883. Sullivan's theatrical appearances and lecture tours brought him in almost $1 million.

Jack O'Brien claimed that he paid Tommy Burns $3500 to lose their world light-heavyweight title bout. 'Burns agreed, knowing that I would ease up in training,' he later claimed. The bout took place in Los Angeles in 1906.

Before it could get under way Burns advanced to the centre of the ring and declared to the crowd, 'Gentlemen, all bets on the fight are off! I agreed to lose to O'Brien, but now we are both in this ring I want to tell you that I am here to win.' Burns won the contest on points.

Tommy Burns insisted on a world record fee of £6000 for defending his heavyweight title against Jack Johnson in Sydney in 1908. He had lost every penny of it on the race tracks by the time he left Australia a few weeks later.

Digger Stanley was only 15 in 1891 when his gypsy father sold him to a boxing booth proprietor for a sovereign and a pot of beer. The young boxer went on to win the world bantamweight championship in 1910.

Charlie Weinert handed out a systematic beating to his heavyweight opponent Bob Roper in Newark in 1920. Realising that he could not win and wishing to get the contest over with quickly, Roper deliberately hit his man low and was disqualified. The incensed crowd threatened to mob Roper. Hastily the boxer seized the microphone. Unctuously he declared that he wished to give value for money. He had been contracted to box 12 rounds, so he would fight the remaining eight with any man in the hall. Unfortunately for the veteran heavyweight, his offer was taken up by a young hopeful sitting in the cheapest seats, Ray Shannon. Shannon went on to give Roper his second beating of the evening.

In 1901 Peggy Bettinson, matchmaker for the National Sporting Club, heard of a promising young bantamweight called Joe Bowker fighting in the Manchester area. He invited the youth to take part in a competition at the club. Bowker had no money so he walked the entire distance to London in ten days, sleeping on the roadside at night. He won the competition which was to launch him on a career which culminated in his winning the world championship in 1904.

When the National Sporting Club in London issued Lonsdale belts to its champions they were made of gold. Any fighter who won a championship bout at the same weight three times kept the belt and was granted a pension of £1 a week when he reached the age of 50.

Mike Donovan defeated Walter Watson in 1884 for a purse and the post of boxing instructor at the New York Athletic Club.

Frank Moran had been swindled by several promoters in his time, so when he was matched against Jack Dillon in Brooklyn in 1916 he demanded his $20 000 purse in advance. On the night of the bout Dillon saw that the hall was half empty, so *he* asked for his $10 000 before he entered the ring. The desperate promoter ransacked the box office and came up with every cent in the house – $8700 in dollars and coins. Dillon and his manager entered the ring carrying the money in the water bucket. A friend of the manager's sat on the bucket throughout the contest to guard the precious contents. The bout was a 10-round no decision.

Manager Steve Ellis took his boxer Chico Vejar to a magistrate's office in New York to pay a total of $650 in fines that Vejar had run up for traffic penalties. To milk the occasion for all it was worth Ellis arranged for photographers and reporters to be present to record Vejar's public-spiritedness. This annoyed the magistrate, who looked up his records and found that Ellis himself owed over $1000 for traffic violations. The manager had to pay before he was allowed to leave with the fighter.

Charlie Mitchell was presented with a gold and silver belt after he had held John L Sullivan to a 39-round draw in France in 1888. When Mitchell's son was killed in World War I, the belt was presented to the British War Museum. It was auctioned for the War Wounded fund.

Penny-pinching heavyweight Jack Sharkey found a way to economise while training for his bout with James J Jeffries in 1899. After a training run on Staten

Island, Sharkey would go into a saloon, buy a nickel beer and then demolish the free lunch set out for patrons. The proprietor got so fed up with being ripped off that after a few days he replaced the free lunch with several sacks of dog-biscuits, and sat back to see how Sharkey would react. As usual the heavyweight came in, bought his beer and headed for the food. He was nonplussed when he saw the dog biscuits, but nevertheless munched his way through most of them. The proprietor gave up and put a proper free lunch on the table the next day. Again Sharkey arrived and headed for the food. He stopped in dismay when he saw the lunch. 'What happened to them cookies?' he demanded.

Jimmy Wilde toured the Rhondda Valley with Jack Scarratt's boxing booth at the beginning of his career. One day the 6½-stone fighter knocked out 17 challengers before tea, which consisted of a cup of tea and a bun. After refreshments he knocked out six more challengers. For the day's work he was paid 15 shillings.

American heavyweight Tex Cobb claimed that his fee for a fight was $10 and a loose woman.

Teofilo Stevenson of Cuba is regarded as the greatest amateur heavyweight of all time. He won Olympic titles at Munich in 1972, Montreal in 1976 and Moscow in 1980. He also won the world amateur heavyweight championship on several occasions. He was offered $2 million dollars by American promoters to turn professional and fight Muhammad Ali, but rejected all inducements to leave Cuba, where professional boxing was banned.

The most highly rewarded of all professional boxers was world welterweight, light-middleweight and middleweight champion Sugar Ray Leonard. By 1991 his total ring earnings were announced as $110 million.

When Wilfred Benitez lost to Mustafa Hamsho in July 1984, he claimed that he had wanted to lose the bout, so that he could buy his contract back from his manager.

British cruiserweight Tom Berry started his career in a boxing booth in 1928. On his first day at work he fought and defeated 11 opponents. For this he was given the princely sum of two halfpennies and a packet of cigarettes.

Light-heavyweight Harold Johnson once received $5000 for not fighting: Archie Moore was scheduled to defend his championship against Italian Giulio Rinaldi but there were grave doubts about Moore's ability to make the weight, so the promoters paid Johnson to stand by to fight Rinaldi. In the event Moore made the weight and outpointed Rinaldi in their 1961 bout in New York.

*'His hand will be fine –
but whose wall is it?'*

Iron Hague held the British heavyweight title for a short while at the beginning of the century. As a young man he would strike a brick wall with his bare fist for a halfpenny.

Youngster Willie Pep received $3 a day for acting as sparring partner to Manuel Ortiz. Six years later, in 1944, he outpointed Ortiz over ten rounds in Boston and received a purse of $20 000.

Jack Johnson knocked Stanley Ketchel out in 12 rounds in Colma, California in 1909, hitting him so hard that after the bout several of Ketchel's front teeth were found embedded in Johnson's glove. Later that night Ketchel took $700 off Johnson in a crap game.

When manager 'Pop' Foster died he left his boxer Jimmy McLarnin his entire fortune of several hundred thousand dollars.

The record loss for a heavyweight championship bout was sustained in the Gene Tunney–Tom Heeney bout in New York in 1928. The gross gate was $691 014. State and federal taxes came to $142 148. The hire of the ballpark cost $50 000. Tickets, advertising and incidental expenses amounted to $60 000. The champion Tunney was paid $525 000, while Heeney received $100 000. Promoter Tex Rickard admitted to a loss of $200 000.

Former world heavyweight champion Jack Dempsey received a then record fee of $10 000 to referee a bout between Ceferino Garcia and Glen Lee in Los Angeles in 1937. Lee won a ten rounds points decision.

Lightweight Bob Montgomery's fourth encounter with Ike Williams drew an incredible $36 million at the box office. Promoter Mike Jacobs sold war bonds instead of tickets. The fighters received only $1500 each in expenses. Both later fell upon hard times.

In 1931, a young black boy read that Kid Chocolate had earned $75 000 for engaging in a non-title fight. The boy took the ring name of Melody Jackson and was knocked out in three rounds in his first professional bout by Al Iovino in Pennsylvania. Jackson persevered, changed his name to Henry Armstrong and won world championships at three weights – feather, light and welter – as well as boxing a draw for the middleweight title.

The 8000 Tunisian fight fans who paid to see the WBO junior-lightweight title bout between Kamel Bou-Ali and Tyrone Downs waited in vain for four hours for the two fighters to appear. Then it was announced that the contest had been cancelled; there was not enough money to pay the two boxers. Later the promoter was arrested for fraud.

Sir Harry Preston was one of the co-promoters of the world middleweight championship bout between American Micky Walker and Scotland's Tommy Milligan in London in 1927. Before the bout he offered odds of 3–1 against the American. Doc Kearns, Walker's manager, took the bet and placed Walker's entire purse on his man, a sum of $120 000. Walker won in ten rounds and took a total of almost $500 000 – his purse plus winnings.

Peter Corcoran, the gigantic Irish heavyweight, stopped his opponent Bill Darts with a single punch for the British heavyweight title in 1771. Captain J O'Kelly, Corcoran's wealthy backer, earned many thousands of pounds in wagers. There were rumours that Darts had sold out for a few hundred pounds to aid the betting coup.

World heavyweight champion Joe Louis, who held the title from 1937 to 1950 and lost only three of 70 bouts, earned over $4½ million during his career. Yet when he retired he had nothing and owed the US Government over $1 million in taxes.

At a court hearing in 1990, it was revealed that former heavyweight champion Mike Tyson had only $15 million left of the $100 million he had earned in the ring.

Before Bill Beynon, a Welsh bantamweight, fought Johnny Hughes in 1913, the promoter Jimmy White was informed by Hughes that he would not enter the ring unless he was paid in advance. White had to wander among the spectators at the ringside, borrowing money from them, in order to pay the boxer. The two men fought a draw.

Pay at the gate . . .
and at ringside

I COULDN'T HAVE PUT IT BETTER!

When heavyweight champion John L Sullivan was asked his advice by a young man his reply was terse in the extreme: 'Keep out of politics and learn to box!'

Leach Cross, the 'Fighting Dentist', won few fans with his ruthless fighting style in the opening decades of the 20th century. The lightweight was under no illusions as to his popularity. 'Half the crowd wants to see me killed,' he once remarked. 'The other half wants to bury me!'

In 1919, the highly-regarded lightweight Willie Ritchie interrupted his honeymoon to fight champion Benny Leonard in Newark, New Jersey. It was a big mistake. Leonard knocked out his young challenger in eight rounds. Afterwards the champion had a few words to say about the timing of Ritchie's title quest. 'A young fighter just married is never any good,' said Leonard safely. 'He is romantically inclined just after marriage and not fit for breaking another guy's nose. He loves everybody!'

At a New York enquiry in 1912 held by the Boxing Commission, efforts were made to discover why world featherweight champion Abe Attell had not performed too energetically over a 12 round no-decision bout with Kayo Brown. In the course of a cross-examination the serious-minded Brown was asked what Attell had said to him when he entered the ring. 'He said, "Hello, you silly-looking bum!"' explained Brown gravely.

After Bombardier Billy Wells, the British heavyweight, had been knocked out in 73 seconds by French light-heavyweight Georges Carpentier in London in 1913, the Welsh featherweight Jim Driscoll was so disgusted by the Englishman's poor showing that he rushed to the ringside to shower the stricken boxer with abuse. Lord Lonsdale had to leave his ringside seat and escort the incensed Welshman away.

Mike Gibbons, 'the St Paul Phantom', so outclassed his opponent Augie Ratner over ten rounds in New York in 1921 that between rounds Ratner looked up blearily at his manager Doc Bagley and begged between puffed lips, 'Do me a favour. After this, match me with only one guy at a time!'

When a number of new weight divisions were introduced in the USA between the wars, the boxing establishment in Great Britain was enraged. Matters came to a head in 1930 when London's Jack 'Kid' Berg was matched with American Mushy Callahan for the latter's junior-welterweight title at the Albert Hall. When the MC started to introduce the bout, no less a figure than Lord Lonsdale rose to his feet and protested angrily that there was no such thing as a junior-welterweight class. Berg's manager, the American Sol Gold, yelled at the peer, 'Sit down, you Limey SOB!' Reluctantly Lord Lonsdale took his seat and the bout got under way. Berg won the title on a stoppage.

There was a certain lordly air about world light-heavyweight champion Archie Moore when he defended his title against Yolande Pompey at Harringay Arena in 1956. In the second round the referee demanded a little more action from the lethargic champion. Moore was affronted. 'Do you know that you are addressing a world champion?' he demanded with hauteur. 'I am very grieved to be spoken to in this manner. Please do not do it again.' After he had stopped his opponent in ten rounds, Moore gave his multi-coloured bathrobe to J Onslow Fane, President of the British Boxing Board of Control. 'I want the Duke to have it,' said Moore. 'I'm not a Duke,' stammered Onslow Fane. 'Then you should be,' replied Moore.

The term 'fight fan' is derived from the Fancy, the name given to the aristocratic backers of the early prize ring.

As evidence of his reformation, Billy Isaac, a British heavyweight prospect of the 1990s, pointed out the sacrifices he was making for his sport: 'My idea of a good night out was 12 pints of lager, a fight in the car park, wreck a curry house, and then pull an old bird. They were great times, but I've calmed down now.'

Trainer John Davenport did not think that English fight followers valued his charge Lennox Lewis highly enough. 'I think God decided to put all the stupid people in one place,' he declared. 'So he put them in England.'

Rocky Graziano, colourful middleweight title holder, claimed to have received little joy from his tenure as champion. 'A title ain't worth the headaches it brings you,' he complained. 'The commissions are always after you for something when you've got the title. People who wouldn't care if you were alive or dead if you weren't the champion start digging up all sorts of stuff about you that happened years ago. They won't let you fight a guy you might draw dough with. All my troubles started when I became champ.'

When manager Jack Hurley took over the affairs of unsuccessful light-heavyweight Harry Matthews, he told the boxer that he would charge him 50% of his ring earnings. The scandalised Matthews pointed out that other managers charged only a third of a boxer's purse. 'How much are you earning now?' asked Hurley. 'Nothing,' confessed Matthews. 'Well, half of nothing ain't much,' pointed out the manager. Matthews signed the contract.

TERMS OF THE TRADE

HOUSE FIGHTER .... A boxer with connections with the promoter, expected to win

OPPONENT .... Someone brought in to provide opposition for the house fighter, not expected to win

SPOILER .... A boxer with an unattractive style who tends to make his opponents look bad as well

CLUTCHER .... A spoiler who clinches a great deal

NOBBINS .... Money thrown into the ring by patrons after a good bout

DOING A JOB .... Boxing efficiently

HEART .... Courage

TAKING A DIVE .... Pretending to be knocked out

The unorthodox style of Maxie Rosenbloom completely bewildered top contender Dave Shade during their Long Island contest, and the experienced fighter lost unexpectedly to the eccentric youngster. When asked what he thought of Rosenbloom's style, Shade growled, 'He's so . . . wrong, he's right.'

Leading American lightweights Lou Ambers and Tony Canzoneri used to spar together in a New York gymnasium. The serious-minded Ambers was always distressed by his spar-mate's practice of lighting up a cigar after a training session. 'You shouldn't smoke,' he would chide the other boxer. When in 1936 Ambers outlasted Canzoneri to take the world championship from him, the new title-holder visited Canzoneri in his dressing room after the bout. 'You know, Tony,' he said, 'I always told you not to smoke those cigars.'

Barney Ross, world welterweight champion, walked into such a potent right hand from Ceferino Garcia in San Francisco that he blacked out. He came round in the interval between the fifth and sixth rounds to hear his manager Art Winch demanding anxiously, 'Who am I?' 'I know you, Art,' replied the wobbly Ross. 'Then why didn't you answer me before?' asked the manager. 'I've been asking you the same question every round since the first!' Ross recovered well enough to take a narrow points decision.

Former bare-knuckle champion Ned Donnelly became a noted tutor of boxers as well as a promoter of contests. One evening in 1885, he was leaving his club with a young lady when they were attacked by a thug. Donnelly calmly floored his assailant, remarking, 'That's a bit of overtime!' His companion then removed her shoe and struck the prostrate thug several hard blows with the heel. Her action so impressed the 'Professor' that he later married her.

New York promoter William Buckley had a long-standing feud with journalists who panned his tournaments. When several

'A perfect right hook – I think I'm in love!'

newspapers commented on the number of dubious characters attending his promotions, the enraged Buckley entered the ring at the next show and made an announcement. 'Everybody watch your valuables,' he said tersely. 'We have pickpockets and newspapermen present.'

When promoter Phil Lewis surveyed the sparse attendance at one of his promotions at the Lyceum Theatre in Paterson, despite it including world middleweight champion Mike O'Dowd against Billy Kramer, he expressed his displeasure as he was introducing the main event. 'Tonight I'm bringing you a world champion,' he spat. 'But the house is lousy.' The promoter pointed at Kramer. 'This bum has held me up for more money. Just so as I wouldn't disappoint you, I'm giving it to him.' The promoter then indicated O'Dowd. 'Now, if this bum doesn't knock that bum out, he ain't going to get paid!' O'Dowd must have taken the strictures to heart, because he knocked Kramer out in three rounds.

Fritzie Zivic, talking of tough-guy opponent Lew Jenkins, said, 'He was the only guy I knew who could start a fight in an empty room!'

Welsh middleweight Tom Thomas hoped to entice American Willie Lewis into the ring with him. While fighting an exhibition bout, with Lewis in the audience, Thomas did his best to put on an inept performance and lull Lewis into a sense of false security. 'Am I looking bad enough?' the Welshman asked his seconds anxiously between rounds.

After John L Sullivan, former world heavyweight champion, retired from the ring he decided to buy a farm, so while touring with a vaudeville show he inspected a farm outside St Louis. The estate was extremely hilly, and the out-of-condition and rather intoxicated Sullivan grew more and more morose as he trudged up and down the steep inclines. Suddenly he lost his footing, fell and rolled down one of the hills. The farmer peered down at him. 'My farm ends down there,' he pointed out acidly. Sullivan glared back up at his host. 'Then I fell off your damned farm and I'm going to stay off!' he roared.

The terrible beating that Joe Louis handed out to challenger 'Two Ton' Tony Galento in their 1939 world heavyweight championship fight did nothing to diminish the roly-poly Galento's self-confidence. As his seconds and the referee supported his bleeding frame, the challenger was still shouting, 'Let me get at the bum. I can beat him any day!'

For years Galento pestered former heavyweight champion Jack Dempsey to manage him, but Dempsey would have none of it. Still Galento persisted. Eventually Dempsey, now in middle age, had had enough. He invited Galento to spar with him in Stillman's gym and gave the roly-poly boxer a good hiding, finally flooring him. Then Dempsey glared down at his dazed opponent. 'That's how you do it, Tony,' he said. 'Now find yourself a new manager.'

When Najib Daho lost a controversial bout to Ian McLeod at Belle Vue, Manchester, in 1985, Daho's manager Jack Trickett wrote a courteous letter to *Boxing News* in which he wished all the best to the referee – and his seeing-eye dog!

When Bert Cooper put up unexpectedly tough resistance against world champion Evander Holyfield after taking the bout at six days' notice at Atlanta, Georgia in 1991, the challenger observed, 'I was surprised at how good I was and how not so good Holyfield was.'

Hen Pearce, the 'Game Chicken', put up such a show of scientific bare-knuckle fighting against opponent Steven Carte in 1805 that after Carte had recovered consciousness he staggered over to Pearce and said, 'I'm not ashamed of you beating me, Harry, because you are a lot cleverer than anybody I have seen or heard of. Half the time I didn't know what you were at!'

Two novice heavyweights, Jackson and Brewer, fought in Sydney in 1890, each having his first bout. Jackson retired with a broken wrist after two minutes. Brewer then foolishly challenged the great Australian fighter Larry Foley, who was standing in the crowd. Reluctantly Foley took up the challenge and knocked Brewer out with the first punch he threw. Afterwards, commenting on Brewer's three-minute career, Foley said drily, 'He stayed in the game too long!'

After an unsuccessful career, Jersey Joe Walcott had practically retired in 1945 when manager Felix Bocchiccio offered to take him on. The poverty-stricken Walcott indicated an empty coal bin in a corner of his icy-cold living room. 'Keep that filled and I'll fight for you,' he promised grimly. Bocchiccio guided Walcott to the world heavyweight championship.

Yankee Schwartz was talking of his 1912 fight with Willie Ritchie in Cleveland, which he lost in two rounds. 'The first two times I was knocked down I said to myself, "Get up, get up, think what the guys back in Philadelphia will say." The third time he knocked me down I said, "To hell with the guys in Philadelphia; this guy hits too hard, I'm staying on the floor!"'

Willy Pastrano was falling behind in his defence of his world light-heavyweight championship against Terry Downes in England in 1964. Between rounds trainer Angelo Dundee smacked Pastrano hard. The enraged Pastrano raised his fist. 'Don't get mad with me!' spat Dundee. He indicated Downes. '*He's* taking your title away from you. Get mad with *him*!' Pastrano went out and stopped Downes.

Charlie Mitchell inadvertently trod on the foot of John L Sullivan in their bare-knuckle bout at Chantilly in France in 1888. 'Try to fight like a gentleman, you — —,' growled Sullivan.

George Foreman pulled off an upset win when he floored champion Joe Frazier six times to win the world heavyweight title in two rounds in Jamaica in 1972. Muhammad Ali, who had been waiting for a lucrative rematch with Frazier, was asked what he thought when he saw Foreman demolish Frazier. 'I thought, "Oh-oh, there goes a lot of money,"' replied Ali.

In December 1991, Rafael Pineda knocked out Roger Mayweather in Reno in the ninth round. When Mayweather came round he tottered over to the referee, Mills Lane, and asked him what had happened. 'You got hit with a left hook right on the button, Rog,' explained the referee kindly.

BACKROOM BOYS

The first stands ever erected for a prize fight were put up for the Tom Spring–Jack Langan contest outside Worcester in 1824. The builders guaranteed the fighters half the proceeds if they fought in front of the stands, which were packed at 10 shillings per patron. Spring won in 77 rounds.

In 1877, Scottish-born John Knifton defended his British heavyweight championship against Tom Scrutton in London for a purse of £25. The bout was a tough one. The spectators became so excited that fighting broke out in the hall in the ninth round. In an effort to restore order the owner of the hall turned out the gas-lights, leaving the arena in darkness. When the lights went up again it was discovered that the referee, Mr J Jenn, had gone home. The match was called off.

Tom Allen, the bare-knuckle heavyweight champion of America, was hired to scrutinise the tickets of patrons boarding a barge which would take them from Hardscrabble Levée in Pittsburgh to see the Billy Edwards–Sam Collyer lightweight bout in 1869. Allen did not waste time on gatecrashers. Any man without a ticket was thrown over the side into the river.

Australian featherweight Young Griffo would do anything to avoid training. He would go off with his dog on a training run, and when the pair of them returned the dog would be panting with exhaustion. One day Griffo's trainer crept after his charge. He found Griffo sitting under a tree throwing sticks for the dog to retrieve! After that, the trainer always accompanied Griffo on his runs, riding a bicycle.

The 25-round draw fought between featherweights Abe Attell and Owen Moran in 1908 satisfied neither participant. Each demanded a return match. Owen wanted the second fight to be over 25 rounds, which would suit his reserves of stamina, while Abe stuck out for the shorter 20-round distance. The promoter compromised on a 23-round bout, the only time this distance has been scheduled for a world title fight. The result was again a draw.

Promoter Hugh D McIntosh gambled everything when he built a stadium at Rushcutter's Bay, Sydney and guaranteed Jack Johnson $5000 and Tommy Burns $30 000 to fight for the latter's heavyweight title. McIntosh put his trust in the US Navy, which was on a goodwill tour to Australia at the time. If no one else came, thought McIntosh, at least the sailors would buy tickets. In the event only two sailors in uniform turned up. They started fighting and had to be evicted. Fortunately some 20 000 Australians watched the bout, giving the promoter a profit of $50 000.

Everden is 'disqualified' . . .

Chatham welterweight Arthur Everden found himself in trouble with the referee at Dieppe in 1912 when he fought a French opponent. Throughout the contest the referee kept hitting Everden sharply on the arm as a signal for the Englishman to break clear. After a few rounds Everden was in such agony from the barrage of slaps and pokes from the official that he turned and struck the referee on the jaw. The referee picked the welterweight up and threw him out of the ring. When the dazed Everden crawled back in under the ropes the referee disqualified him.

Broadway Charlie Rose was considered one of the shrewdest of fight managers. In 1914 he was seconding Freddy Welsh in a bout against Joe Shugrue at Madison Square Garden. At the end of the third round Rose dashed into the ring to attend to his fighter. In the process he caught a ring on his finger against a spike used to tighten the ring ropes, sustaining a bad injury. Blood gushed from the wound, soaking Welsh, who had not been touched by his opponent. Not taking kindly to being coated in his manager's blood, Welsh tried to push Rose out of the ring. Desperate to perform his duties in the corner Rose started slapping at his fighter. In the end several policemen had to escort him, protesting wildly, out of the ring, while the crowd cheered. Welsh outpointed his opponent in a fight far duller than the goings-on in his corner before the fourth round.

A tragedy was only narrowly averted when Johnny Weber lost his Minnesotan featherweight title to Jackie Nichols in 1926. An excited second poured smelling salts instead of water down Weber's throat between rounds. The boxer collapsed. He was ill for months and had to retire from the ring.

Robert Barclay was the leading boxing trainer of the 19th century. He was charged with preparing the overweight Tom Cribb for his return bout with the black American Tom Molineaux in 1811. The trainer chased his charge over the Scottish hills, throwing pebbles at him to make him run faster. Cribb shed three stone in ten weeks and defeated his opponent with ease.

Cribb's better off with trainer Barclay

'This'll soon put you right'

Georges Carpentier took America by storm when he arrived in 1921 to challenge Jack Dempsey for the world heavyweight championship. In the dressing rooms before the contest, promoter Tex Rickard was struck by the difference in the physiques of the two fighters. He realised that the Frenchman just did not possess the bulk to mount a serious challenge to the champion. Rickard hurried to Dempsey's dressing room and begged the champion not to knock Carpentier out with the first punch. 'People have paid a fortune to see this fight,' he implored, referring to the 80 000 spectators who had paid almost $2 million. 'Let it go a few rounds.' Dempsey's reply was just a grunt. He outclassed the Frenchman and flattened him in four rounds in their Jersey City encounter. 'I should have known,' sighed Rickard afterwards. 'Jack wouldn't have carried his own brother once that bell rang!'

Billy Miske was a leading contender for the world heavyweight title in the years after World War I, but later fell upon hard times. In 1920 he lost most of his savings when his automobile business failed. He was then diagnosed as suffering from cancer, and retired from the ring. By 1923 he was unable to support his wife and three children. He begged his former manager to get him just one last fight, so that his family could have one good Christmas together. Reluctantly his manager matched him with heavyweight Bill Brennan for a bout on 7 November. Miske was too ill to train, so he merely rested at home. He knocked Brennan out in four rounds, earning a purse of $2400. His manager refused to

take his percentage and the fighter was able to give his family the Christmas he had dreamt about. On 26 December he was admitted into hospital and he died a week later on New Year's Day, 1924.

Jack Sharkey won the world heavyweight championship, but he was always a temperamental fighter. In his 1931 contest with the gigantic Italian Primo Carnera he knocked his opponent down halfway through the bout. Carnera staggered to his feet at the count of nine but Sharkey was convinced that his adversary had not beaten the count. When the referee would not agree with his proposition, Sharkey stormed to the ropes in a huff and tried to leave the ring. His portly manager Johnny Buckley pulled himself up onto the apron and hustled around outside the ropes. Every time that Sharkey tried to duck underneath the strands, Buckley would push his fighter back. In the end Sharkey gave up the unequal encounter and turned round and resumed hitting Carnera, regarding this as being the easier option. He won on points over 15 rounds.

British heavyweight Jack Petersen was a promoter's dream. Handsome and charismatic, he topped the bill for each of his professional contests and no promoter ever made a loss on a tournament in which Petersen appeared.

Fiery Liverpool-born manager James J Johnston once organised a heavyweight tournament in

New York to find a likely contender. Over a hundred hopefuls entered. The manager was so disgusted at the standards displayed that he wanted to bet that he could beat any of the giants in the ring.

In 1935 Max Schmeling and Walter Neusel, two prominent German heavyweights, refused, after many warnings, to discharge their Jewish managers. Joe Jacobs, Schmeling's manager, was particularly censured for giving the Nazi salute from the ring with a cigar smoking between the fingers of his extended hand. When he returned to the USA, Jacobs walked into another storm from American Jews for giving the salute at all. Jacobs excused himself by saying that he had crossed the fingers of his other hand behind his back.

Yale graduate and Rhodes Scholar Eddie Eagan won the light-heavyweight gold medal at the Antwerp Olympics and sparred exhibition contests with professional heavyweight champion Jack Dempsey. In the 1932 Winter Olympics Eagan won another gold medal, this time as a member of the US four-man bobsleigh team. He was the only athlete to win gold medals at both the Summer and Winter Olympics. Later he became Chairman of the New York State Athletic Commission. Here he engaged in a number of well-publicised disputes with hard-nosed former Army deserter Rocky Graziano, the middleweight champion, who had little time for the aristocratic 'Colonel'.

Handsome Steve Hamas, a graduate of Pennsylvania State University, was a leading contender for the world heavyweight championship in 1935 until he went to Hamburg to fight Max Schmeling. A horrified crowd saw Hamas take a terrible beating. When the American's manager was asked why he had not thrown in the towel, he said that it was not the American tradition to give in and that he had been waiting for the referee to stop the fight. Hamas was knocked out in the ninth round. He never fought again.

Battling Levinsky was an experienced fighter but on the night he met Joe Louis in Chicago in 1935 his legs turned to water and he could hardly stand before his open-air bout with the up and coming black fighter at Comiskey Park. A good hour before the bout was scheduled to begin, he was in a terrible state. The shrewd promoter dashed out before Levinsky actually fainted. It was a cloudless night but the promoter persuaded a bewildered official that rain was imminent and got Levinsky's bout brought forward while the boxer could still be half-carried into the ring. Louis won in the first round.

Boxing enthusiast Frank Churchill went to work in the Philippines early in the 20th century. He was so impressed with the fighting ability of the islanders that he managed three of them to success, only to see all three of his boxers die in tragic circumstances. In 1921, his featherweight hope Dencio Cabanella collapsed and died while fighting Bert McCarthy in Australia. Four years later, his world flyweight champion Pancho Villa boxed Jimmy McLarnin while suffering from a poisoned tooth in Oakland, California. Villa lost the bout, collapsed and died ten days later. A year later, the third of Churchill's fighters, Inocencio Moldes, died after fighting Bud Taylor in Milwaukee.

Scottish fighter Alex Farries tried to save money by riding his motor-bike to Dundee for a contest. The promoter reduced his purse from £4 to £2.10s because the boxer had not come by train.

In November 1950, former British heavyweight champion Tommy Farr had the second of his comeback fights after a ten year lay-off. Farr knocked out Piet Wilde of Belgium in the third round, but only after some difficulty. The referee and the timekeeper were both over 70 years of age. It was alleged that the final count over the prostrate Wilde was a shambles, with the officials totally unable to synchronise their counts.

The organisers of the international heavyweight bout between Frank Bruno and American Tim Witherspoon in London in July 1986 delayed the start until 1am to meet the requirements of American television.

World middleweight champion Ray Robinson could never be regarded as a loner. On his boxing tour of Europe in 1951 he took a staff of 11 with him. In addition to his wife, he had on the payroll a secretary, a golf partner, a singing and tap-dancing hairdresser, a trainer and other luminaries. When questioned about this, George Gainford, Robinson's manager, said indignantly, 'There are no clowns in the camp. Every man in our employ has a special job to do.'

When he felt that his son Sean was slipping as a lightweight, manager Pat O'Grady formed his own governing body, the World Athletic Association, and declared that son Sean was its lightweight title holder. He also appointed his son-in-law Monte Masters to be the WAA heavyweight champion. When Monte had a domestic tiff with O'Grady's daughter, Pat promptly stripped his errant son-in-law of his 'title'.

American manager Lou Duva may have been 70 years old in 1988, but when he felt that featherweight Roger Mayweather had handled Duva's protegé a little harshly, the veteran manager stormed over and hit Mayweather. The boxer struck back, cutting Duva's cheek. The Nevada Boxing Commission suspended Duva for ungentlemanly conduct.

Manager Ancel Hoffman was instrumental in getting his own fighter Buddy Baer disqualified against Joe Louis in their fight for the world heavyweight title in Washington in 1941. Early in the

'. . . and to the BBBC, I leave one penny'

bout Baer knocked Louis out of the ring, but the champion returned to give the enormous challenger a thrashing. At the end of the sixth round Louis hit Baer as the bell sounded. Hoffman insisted that his fighter had been struck after the bell and that the champion should be disqualified. When Hoffman refused to let Buddy Baer leave his corner, the referee disqualified Baer.

Jack Solomons was Britain's leading promoter in the post-war era. He had a stormy relationship with the authorities. After his death it was announced in his will that he had left the British Boxing Board of Control the sum of one penny.

W Warren Barbour became a US Senator for New Jersey. As a young amateur boxer he was advised to turn professional by former world heavyweight champion James J Corbett, but refused to leave the unpaid ranks. He accepted the position of timekeeper when Jess Willard defended his heavyweight championship against Jack

Dempsey in Toledo in 1919. Dempsey's manager had bet his fighter's entire purse that he would knock Willard out in the first round. Dempsey floored the champion half a dozen times in the first three minutes, and the referee actually counted Willard out. Barbour managed to attract the official's attention and inform him that the bell had rung before he had reached the count of 'ten'. The fight was resumed and Dempsey won in three rounds, but he had lost his purse money in the bet.

Glen Flanagan outpointed Pat Iacobucci at Hibbing, Minnesota in 1951, then walked over to his opponent's corner and hit Iacobucci's manager Eddie Johnson. 'He was riding me all through the fight,' explained Flanagan sourly afterwards.

American manager Leo P Flynn wanted to take on promising young fighter Billy Shade in 1921. However, Shade's father insisted that the manager look after Billy's younger brother Dave as well. Flynn was reluctant to do this, but he wanted Billy badly so he agreed to manage Dave too. Billy never amounted to much as a boxer, but Dave went on to become a leading middleweight.

Anne Morgan, daughter of American millionaire J Pierpont Morgan, promoted a successful boxing tournament in 1921. As the organiser of the 'Fund for Devastated France' she was eager to raise money to help rebuild France after the war. She hit upon the idea of arranging a world

lightweight title fight between Benny Leonard and Richie Mitchell. The event was both a social and a financial success. The charity received $75 000 and Leonard retained his title on a sixth round knockout.

A crocodile park in Thailand was the unusual arena chosen by the promoter of the Khaosai Galaxy–Jae-suk Pak championship bout. The contest went ahead even after the promoter had been murdered the day before the event. Galaxy won in five rounds.

Former world lightweight champion Battling Nelson was scheduled to referee a bout between Packy O'Gatty and Benny Coster at the Pioneer Club in New York. Nelson became involved with some of the crowd who objected to his decisions in the ring. While O'Gatty and Coster continued with the bout behind him, Nelson strode to the ropes and spent the rest of the round challenging anyone in the audience to come up and fight him.

Mike Collins, the editor of a boxing magazine, in 1922 organised a poll among his readers to see who they thought should be the first champion at the newly formed light-welterweight limit. The fighter securing the most votes was Pinkie Mitchell. Surprisingly, Mitchell was managed by editor Collins. Not so surprisingly, Mitchell lost the title the first time he defended it – against Mushy Callahan, four years later.

'Victor? I think
I found us a champ!'

A California promoter was so
impressed when he saw boxers
Art Aragon and Laura Salas
brawling in a bar that he signed
them up for a genuine contest in
1951. The official fight was
almost as good as the
spontaneous one had been, with
Aragon gaining a split decision
over ten rounds.

CELEBRITY BOXERS

SIR ARTHUR CONAN DOYLE
The 6ft 2in author of the Sherlock Holmes stories was a keen amateur boxer. On his first day as a doctor in Southsea he knocked out a labourer who was kicking his wife. The chastened navvy later became a patient of the 15-stone doctor. Conan Doyle wrote what is probably the greatest of all novels of the prize-ring, *Rodney Stone*. He was even considered as a possible referee for the world heavyweight championship bout between Jack Johnson and James J Jeffries at Reno in 1910.

GEORGE BERNARD SHAW
As an unsuccessful young writer in London towards the end of the 19th century, the future author of *Pygmalion* took boxing lessons from former champion Ned Donnelly at the latter's gymnasium. In his book *Shaw's Champions* (Elm Tree Books), Benny Green reveals that Shaw actually entered for the middleweight and heavyweight classes in the Amateur Championships in 1883, but that he was not selected to compete.

MAURICE BARRYMORE
An Englishman who had considerable success on the New York stage towards the end of the 19th century, he was the father of three children who became outstanding actors of the American stage and screen, John, Ethel and Lionel. Maurice was a keen amateur boxer who claimed to have won the lightweight championship of England as an amateur while a student at Oxford University.

GEORGE O'BRIEN
Film star O'Brien played the lead in the epic silent western *The Iron Horse* in 1924 and went on to star in the classic *Sunrise* and one of the first epics, *Noah's Ark*. His publicity hand-outs declared, 'He's a Man's Man and an Idol of Women'. Before that, during a two-year stint as a sailor, O'Brien had won the championship of the Pacific Fleet as a boxer. Jack Dempsey's manager Doc Kearns offered to take O'Brien on as a professional, but then the young actor secured the lead in *The Iron Horse*, the 58th aspirant to be tested for the role.

When former heavyweight champion Jack Dempsey promoted a bout between Max Baer and Max Schmeling in 1935, he secured a great deal of publicity for the bout by boxing with both contestants in training sessions.

Norvel Lee was beaten in the trials for the US Olympic boxing team in 1952, but was with the team as assistant trainer when the selected light-heavyweight was injured. Lee took off 19 pounds in weight, won the gold medal and was given the trophy as the best boxer of the entire competition.

Manager Charlie Rose thought he had discovered a potential heavyweight champion when he took on 6ft 6in Jack Pettifer, who came into boxing from washing up in the kitchen of a Lyons' corner-house in London. Pettifer was as strong as an ox, but had moral scruples about hitting people smaller than himself. As he dwarfed most of his opponents, this turned out to be an insurmountable problem, even for the experienced Rose. Pettifer got as far as an unsuccessful title shot against Jack Petersen, but Rose gave him up as being altogether too soft-hearted ever to become a champion.

Larry Gaines, a black Canadian heavyweight, was good enough to defeat Primo Carnera, who became heavyweight champion of the world. As a young fighter in Paris after the First World War, Gaines was managed by a young reporter who was trying to become a novelist – Ernest Hemingway.

Famous Western gunslinger and occasional lawman Bat Masterton refereed and acted as timekeeper in a number of important heavyweight bouts towards the end of the 19th century. Later he became a boxing writer for the New York *Morning Telegraph*.

OOPS, SORRY!

When 19-year-old Bombardier Billy Wells won the Indian Army heavyweight title in 1909, many thought he was a likely professional prospect. He was given a trial behind closed doors against British heavyweight champion Gunner Moir. For two rounds the lanky Wells boxed rings round the champion, but then walked into a right hand and was knocked out. Wells had impressed enough people for him to be bought out of the army and launched on a paid career. He rattled off a string of impressive victories and was then matched with Moir in public. Again Wells boxed his opponent silly and again he walked into a right hand and was knocked out in the third round.

Harry Mayo and Archie Davies were engaged in an eight round contest in Australia in 1951. As he circled the ring Mayo heard the ringside radio commentator describing the action. He stopped to hear how he was getting on and Davies staggered him with a hard left hook. Mayo recovered to win on points.

'Mayo's controlling this fight no problem at all . . .'

'He won't get up
from that one'

The Manhattan Opera House was the unlikely venue for a boxing tournament in 1916. Heavyweight André Anderson met Charley Weinert in a ring on the stage of the theatre. A number of musical instruments were stored in the orchestra pit.

In the second round Weinert knocked Anderson out of the ring and into the pit. The dazed heavyweight landed in the mouth of the big bass horn and was unable to extricate himself before the count of ten.

Amateur welterweight Rich Keeling knocked out Bill Redford in Louisville in 1952, only to be flattened in turn by Redford's mother, who jumped into the ring and caught Keeling with a right swing.

When heavyweight Pat Comiskey hit opponent Joe Kahut in their fight at Portland, Oregon in 1951, Kahut's shorts split and dropped to the floor.

American heavyweight Joe Baksi made a big mistake when he agreed to fight Olle Tandberg in Stockholm in 1947. Baksi had just hammered British heavyweight champion Bruce Woodcock and was slated to fight Joe Louis for the world title. After defeating Woodcock, Baksi spent some

'That's for my boy!'

time relaxing in Europe. In order to pick up some loose change he agreed to fight the Swede Tandberg before returning to the USA and finalising arrangements for the Louis bout. Baksi was badly out of condition and lost on points to the Swede. There was no way that promoter Mike Jacobs could put Louis in against a loser, so Joe Walcott got the title shot instead. Baksi lost another fight, this time to Ezzard Charles, and was ruled out of contention as a contender.

Some unusual accidents have occurred in training sessions, but only triple world champion Henry Armstrong was knocked out by his own shadow. While preparing for his 1938 welterweight bout against Ceferino Garcia, Armstrong slipped on a rug during a shadow-boxing session. He fell, knocking himself out and sustaining a slipped disc. The contest had to be postponed.

Heavyweight challenger Tami Mauriello came along before the era of the permissive society. After Joe Louis had knocked him out in one round in New York in 1946, Mauriello was interviewed live on NBC radio. The challenger blurted out, 'I got too God-damned careless!' Shocked radio executives pulled the plugs at once and replaced the post-fight interviews with a long session of soothing organ music.

An argumentative timekeeper stole the show during the 1948 Madison Square Garden middleweight bout between Frenchman Marcel Cerdan and Lavern Roach. In the second round Cerdan floored Roach, who managed to pull his opponent to the floor with him. Cerdan got up to find the referee in furious dispute with the timekeeper. While Roach lay dazed on the canvas, the timekeeper refused to count him out because, he claimed, Roach had only slipped to the floor. The referee insisted that a punch had floored the middleweight. Finally, with great reluctance, the timekeeper agreed to count in time with the referee. Roach rose at the count of eight, although he had been on his back for at least 24 seconds. Cerdan went on to win by a knockout in round eight.

Oakland Billy Smith gave leading light-heavyweight title contender Archie Moore all the trouble he could handle for eight rounds in their bout at Portland, Oregon in 1951. He even got off the floor to deck Moore for a count. Suddenly, in the middle of the eighth round, Smith turned away from his opponent, leapt out of the ring and fled for the safety of his dressing room, refusing to emerge. Afterwards Moore commented, 'Billy seemed to get kind of discouraged.' All that Smith would say was, 'I got confused!'

French featherweight Ray Famechon was knocked down in the second round by Eddie Burgin in their 1951 Cincinnati contest. He got up and told referee Tony Warnock that he wanted to carry on. Warnock, who spoke no French, thought that Famechon was saying that he was retiring. He stopped the bout.

In a Kansas City bout Pat Kissinger and Al Dorlac rushed at each other at the beginning of the third round. They clashed heads, fell to the canvas and were both counted out.

Film star Errol Flynn claimed to have been a boxer in his youth, and when he was the worse for drink he had a habit of picking on strangers in bars. On one occasion he challenged a middle-aged Red Indian. It was a big mistake. The Red Indian was Jim Thorpe, professional footballer and winner of gold medals in the pentathlon and decathlon at the 1912 Olympics. Thorpe wiped the floor with Flynn.

Mike Holt and Johnny Halafihi met at Nottingham in an eliminator for the Empire light-heavyweight championship in 1960. At the end of the tenth round the referee added up his points and lifted Halafihi's hand as a sign that he had won on points. It was pointed out to the referee that the contest was scheduled for 12 rounds. The final two rounds were then fought and the verdict announced as a draw.

Although Sonny Liston had lost his heavyweight crown to Muhammad Ali, he was still considered almost unbeatable when he was training for his contest with Henry Clarke in 1968. To help him with his preparations he hired an unknown former marine called Mac Foster as a sparring partner. In a training session Foster hit Liston so hard on the jaw that the former champion had to be helped back to his corner. He could not move from his stool for at least ten minutes. It was the high spot of the former Marine's fighting career. He went on to lose to Muhammad Ali, Jerry Quarry and a number of others.

Anthony Hembrick of the USA was one of the favourites for a gold medal at the Seoul Olympics. He missed the team bus taking boxers to the stadium and arrived too late for his bout.

Lightweight Kenny Bognor was ahead on points against Edwin Curet in their 1984 bout in Atlantic City when he sustained a cut over one eye. The referee stopped the fight in Curet's favour. A video film of the contest then showed that the cut had been caused by a butt from Curet. The New Jersey Commissioners reversed the decision and gave Bognor a technical victory.

American heavyweight Renaldo Snipes did not have a good evening against heavyweight champion Larry Holmes in Pittsburgh in 1981. In the seventh round he floored the champion, only to see Holmes stagger to his feet and last out the round. Gradually Holmes got on top and stopped Snipes in the 11th round. As the second was cutting the bandages off Snipes' hands, the handler was jostled by the crowd in the ring. The second's hand slipped and the point of the scissors cut a deep wound in Snipes' arm.

Over 1.3 million people saw Joe Frazier outpoint Muhammad Ali on closed circuit television in their 1971 bout at Madison Square Garden. But not at the Chicago Coliseum. The technical apparatus failed and the irate fans wrecked the place.

Amid the celebrations in Micky Walker's dressing room after he had retained his world middleweight championship against Tommy Milligan in London in 1927, manager Doc Kearns gave supporter Walter 'Good Time' Friedman a wad of pound notes and told him to buy tickets for the whole party to go to Dublin the following morning, so that Walker could meet some of his Irish relatives. On the way to the booking office Friedman thought, 'Hell, I don't know anyone in Dublin!' Instead he purchased a block of tickets for Paris. The party spent three days in France, thinking they were in Ireland. When Walker asked

'Er, has anyone got a radio?'

'That was my stool . . .'

about the language he could hear being spoken around him, Friedman assured the boxer that it was Gaelic.

Garth Panter stood up to start the fifth round against Baby Day at San Francisco, realised that there were still a few seconds of rest due to him, and sat down again. It was too late, his seconds had removed his stool. Panter went on to lose on points.

Jorge Muniz was a Mexican pop singer selected to sing the Mexican national anthem before a boxing tournament in Mexico City. Overcome by the occasion he forgot the words. He was fined one million pesos by the authorities.

When Jack Dempsey lost his second bout to Gene Tunney in 1927, Dempsey's chauffeur bet a month's wages on his boss. Unfortunately, without Dempsey's knowledge, he also bet the car.

Joey de John knocked out Henry Kid Lee twice in the same round in Buffalo in 1951. In the third round de John knocked Lee down and the referee tolled the count over him. When Lee staggered to his feet, the official waved his arms to signify that the bout was over. De John thought that the referee was waving the contest on. He stepped in and knocked Lee out again.

The promoter of the bout between Kid Norfolk and Larry Williams in Jersey City suspected that Norfolk might not try too hard. Before the bout he told the Kid that he would not get paid unless he fought his hardest. Norfolk took the warning to heart and knocked Williams out

with the first punch he landed. The promoter almost had a riot on his hands because the bout had ended so quickly.

In February 1990, at East London, South Africa, welterweights Norman Zwilbi and Xolani Sirunhu landed simultaneous left hooks to the jaw. Both fell unconscious to the canvas in a double knockout.

In 1991 newspapers reported the action of a former British heavyweight contender seconding a boxer in a small hall bout. When the buzzer sounded to warn the seconds out of the ring, the ex-boxer automatically put the gum-shield in his own mouth instead of his boxer's.

When Gilbert Dele defended his junior-middleweight title against Vinny Pazienza at Providence in 1991, a recording of the German national anthem *Deutschland Über Alles* was played in his honour. Unfortunately Dele was a Frenchman. He was knocked out in 12 rounds.

Heavyweight champion Jack Dempsey did not serve in the armed forces in World War I. However, he did pose for a publicity shot showing him working in a shipyard, clad in hard-hat and overalls. Unfortunately he was still wearing glossy patent-leather shoes. The photograph was

Larkin's pre-fight entertainment

published in newspapers all over the country and did little for the champion's popularity.

When Tippy Larkin was introduced to the crowd before his contest with Tommy Cross at Newark in 1942 he threw off his robe with a flourish and acknowledged the cheers of the crowd. Then hastily he put the gown back on again. Larkin had forgotten to wear his boxing trunks.

Australian heavyweight George Cook's face was so badly disfigured after his victory over Frank Goddard in 1923 that friends took him home, propped him against the door and ran off before Mrs Cook could open it.

American heavyweight Larry Hooseman split his trunks against Tommy Farr in their 1952 contest in Cardiff. No single replacement pair could be found to fit the boxer's ample frame. Instead he had to wear three pairs of shorts, one over the other. They fitted so snugly that Hooseman was unable to sit down between rounds. He won on points.

In 1808 a succession of exhausted horses took an urgent message from Lord Grey, the Foreign Secretary, to the War Secretary. In each town the lathered horses galloped through, there were rumours that war must be imminent. It turned out that the message being sent 'on public service' was the result of the second contest between John Gully and Bob Gregson, won by Gully at Woburn in eight rounds.

Bobby Ruffin got bored waiting in the dressing room to fight Johnny Greco, so he went for a walk. He got back in time to hear his bout being cancelled because he could not be found. Unhurriedly Ruffin completed his walk by strolling down to the ring and then boxing a draw with Greco.

Two Australian middleweights, Ron Richards and Fred Henneberry, met nine times between 1933 and 1941. Five of their bouts ended in disqualifications. Richards won six bouts, Henneberry won two, and one was a draw.

When referee Eugene Henderson joined the RAF at the beginning of World War II, he was ordered to box an exhibition contest for the benefit of the airmen. When Henderson turned up at the hall he found that his opponent was heavyweight Jack London. Henderson had disqualified London for foul fighting in one of the last contests at which he officiated before joining the air force.

After Johnny Williams had lost narrowly to Jack Gardner in an eliminating contest for the British heavyweight title, he spent the night in hospital suffering from exhaustion. He found himself listening to the man in the next bed complaining loudly and incessantly about the amount of money he had lost by backing Johnny Williams in that evening's big fight.

THAT'S SHOW BUSINESS!

In a Colorado mining town in 1909, a young challenger won a few dollars by lasting six rounds with world middleweight champion Stan Ketchel. The challenger used part of his winnings to buy his son a violin. The boy was Fritz Kreisler, who grew up to become one of the world's greatest violinists.

American light-heavyweight Battling Levinsky loved to fight. Once, he had taken a young lady to the theatre when he was called to the manager's office and told that he was wanted as a last-minute substitute on the other side of New York. Levinsky caught a cab to the stadium, borrowed some boxing gear, knocked out his opponent in two rounds and returned to the theatre in time for the second act.

Former British lightweight champion Dave Crowley made a considerable career as a film stunt man and orchestrated the spectacular fight between John Mills and Stewart Granger in *Waterloo Road*.

Dom Volante, a contender for the British featherweight title, knocked out his opponent in 29 seconds of the first round at Barnsley in 1932. Fearing that the patrons had not had their money's worth, Volante hurried to the dressing room and then returned to the ring carrying a mouth organ. He proceeded to play for the crowd for 30 minutes, the scheduled length of the remaining nine rounds.

Frank Hough, the 'Fighting Hussar', was a real crowd-pleaser in the small halls of London. Something of an all-rounder, he was bought out of the Army to become a full-time fighter. Hough was also a gifted musician, winning one of Carroll Levis' talent contests and joining the Louis Levy orchestra. In 1937 he was given a contract to box once a week for 12 successive weeks at the Empress Stadium in London.

In 1902, the National Sporting Club of London put on a great Carnival of Champions to mark the coronation of King Edward VII. It opened on 21 June and lasted for four days. The tournament opened with a competition for the Greco-Roman wrestling championship of the world. A number of prominent American boxers were also imported. Kid McFadden lost to Ben Jordan of Bermondsey, Joe Walcott defended his welterweight title against American Tommy West, world middleweight champion Tommy Ryan met Johnny Gorman, and two leading American heavyweights Tom Sharkey and Gus Ruhlin met, with the latter winning in 11 rounds. The illness of the King put a damper on the occasion, and the Coronation Tournament was a financial failure.

A number of boxers have made a practice of serenading the audience after a hard-fought contest. Irish flyweight Rinty Monaghan's speciality was *When Irish Eyes Are Smiling*. After he had won the British welterweight title from Henry Hall in 1949, Welshman Eddy Thomas treated the spectators to his rendition of *Bless This House*.

World featherweight champion Barry McGuigan's father Pat once came third in the Eurovision Song Contest. After his son became champion Pat would preface Barry's contests by singing *Danny Boy* from the ring.

Jack Palance was a former heavyweight boxer who made it to Hollywood after understudying Marlon Brando on Broadway in *A Streetcar Named Desire*. He achieved lasting movie fame as the evil, black-garbed gunman in the classic Western *Shane*. Palance had taken up boxing to get out of the mines and was good enough to go the distance with Joe Baksi, later to become a leading contender for Joe Louis's heavyweight crown. A tough hombre and devoted exponent of the Method system of acting, Palance threw himself whole-heartedly into his film roles.

His passion for realism did not always endear him to his fellow actors. When he filmed *Panic in the Streets* with Richard Widmark, he was supposed to knock Widmark out with a prop gun made of rubber. In order to add verisimilitude to the scene,

Palance substituted a real pistol for the rubber one, without telling his co-star. The former heavyweight struck the unsuspecting Widmark so hard over the head that the unfortunate actor was unconscious for twenty minutes. When asked later if he had remonstrated with his fellow actor, Widmark replied, 'Hell no! Palance was the one actor I was afraid of. He could turn on you like a snake!'

Several boxers have acted as stand-ins for major films. In *The Quiet Man*, the fighter brawling with John Wayne across the Irish countryside is former Irish heavyweight champion Martin Thornton, not co-star Victor McLaglen. In the opening shot of *Proud Valley*, the massive black man striding along the road in long-shot is not star Paul Robeson but the Scottish heavyweight Manuel Abrew.

Danny Sewell was a promising British heavyweight until he contracted infantile paralysis and had to retire from the ring. He took up acting and played the part of Bill Sykes in *Oliver* on Broadway. His non-boxing brother George also played Sykes in a touring production of *Oliver* in Britain, as well as taking the lead in a number of television series.

American heavyweight Jack O'Halloran had a more successful screen career than most retired boxers. As a fighter O'Halloran had 76 contests, losing to Ken Norton, George Foreman, Joe

Bugner and Jack Bodell. His screen credits were more impressive, with feature roles in *The Big Sleep* and *Superman 2*.

Ken Norton was the only world heavyweight champion not to win his title in the ring. The WBC stripped Leon Spinks of his title and awarded it to Norton, who had featured parts in several steamy film melodramas like *Mandingo*.

In 1975, actor and occasional nightclub brawler Oliver Reed played the part of Count von Bismarck in the film *Royal Flash*. In one scene he had to spar with John Gully, played by former European heavyweight champion Henry Cooper. Director Richard Lester recounted how in the first take, Oliver Reed, fancying his chances, took a speculative swipe at Cooper, who responded with a smart cuff which shook Reed to his toes. In subsequent takes, Reed adhered strictly to the script.

During the filming of *Rocky IV*, star Sylvester Stallone felt that Dolph Lungren, the gigantic actor playing his Russian opponent, was pulling his punches too much. He ordered Lungren to hit him harder in the fight scene. Lungren obeyed, only to put Stallone into hospital.

Daniel Mendoza was perhaps the first really scientific bare-knuckle fighter. He defeated Sam Martin in 1787 and claimed the championship of England.

Mendoza was the first fighter to manage himself. He was also the first to tour the country on a large scale, with an act which he hoped would attract both men and women. His advertising bill read:

Between the parts, Mr Mendoza, the celebrated pugilist, will display his scientific knowledge of self-defence against a practised pupil, by which he has foiled many an opponent. End of Part 1st: Mr Mendoza will exhibit and lecture upon the scientific skill and method of fighting of those celebrated pugilists Big Ben, Johnson, Broughton, Perrins. End of Part 2nd: there will be displayed others equally skilful in science, Humphries, Ward ,Wood, George the Brewer. The ladies are respectfully informed that there is neither violence nor indecency that can offend the most delicate of their sex: as an affirmation of which Mr Mendoza has, by repeated desire, performed before Their Majesties and the Royal Family. The whole to conclude with Mr Mendoza's own original attitude. Admittance: Boxes and Pit, 2s.; gallery, 1s. To begin precisely at seven o'clock.

Tommy Morrison, who claimed to be a distant relative of John Wayne, was making his way as a professional heavyweight when he was signed for a part in *Rocky V*. In order to heighten the realism of the movie it was decided to film one of Morrison's genuine contests in 1989 and splice footage from it into the *Rocky* movie. Sylvester Stallone and co-star Burt Young worked in Morrison's corner for the bout. The contest turned out to be a dog. Morrison laboured for an unconvincing victory over Lorenzo Canady. None of the 'action' was good enough for the completed film.

One of the great boxing non-events was the promotion put on at the *Yorkshire Grey* in Eltham in October 1990. Only two of the billed fighters turned up and a coach party containing most of the spectators broke down and did not arrive. The show went on before a depleted audience. It consisted of one contest, supplemented by a comedian and an exotic dancer.

In 1990, British heavyweights Gary Mason and Horace Notice were both forced to retire from the ring due to injury. A group of well-meaning fellow fighters recorded a disc in a fund-raising drive for their former colleagues. The title of their recording was *Feel No Pain*. It never made the charts.

Oscar-winning actor James Caan, star of *The Godfather*, seconded heavyweight aspirant Mike 'the Bounty' Hunter in his 1987 bout against Mike Gans in California. Hunter posed for publicity shots in full Western gear, brandishing a six-shooter.

As a public relations exercise, Mexican bandit Pancho Villa tried to stage the Jess Willard–Jack Johnson heavyweight title contest in Mexico. The match fell through when Johnson could not penetrate the government-held coastal strip.

Black middleweight and welterweight Canada Lee became an actor when he gave up boxing in 1938. He had a leading role in the stage play *Native Son*, directed by Orson Welles, and received much critical acclaim for his film roles in *Body and Soul* and *Cry the Beloved Country*.

There was so much interest in the second Gene Tunney–Jack Dempsey bout for the world heavyweight title, held in Chicago in 1927, that two fighters, Berny Hufnagle and Eddie Ross, were hired to simulate the moves of the two heavyweights at the 71st Armoury in New York. Details of the world championship fight were wired to the armoury from Chicago. A telegraph operator provided copies for the seconds, who read them to the New York boxers between rounds. Hufnagle and Ross then went out and duplicated the moves of Dempsey and Tunney. Over 1000 people paid to see this replica of the championship.

American heavyweight Coley Wallace was considered a hot prospect after he twice won the Golden Gloves title and defeated Rocky Marciano as an amateur. Despite some good victories Wallace never really made it as a professional, but he did play the part of the former champion in the film *The Joe Louis Story*.

Young Stribling claimed a total of 286 bouts. Many of these were simulated contests to pad out the fighter's record. Stribling would tour the small towns of the USA with his parents, fighting his chauffeur under a variety of names.

Many world champions adopted a ring name which was easier for the announcer to pronounce than their real one.

REAL NAME	RING NAME	TITLE
Noah Brusso	Tommy Burns	Heavyweight 1906–08
George Chipulonis	George Chip	Middleweight 1913–14
Stanislaus Kiecal	Stanley Ketchel	Middleweight 1907–08, 1908–10
Aaron L Brown	Dixie Kid	Welterweight 1904
Norman Selby	Kid McCoy	Welterweight 1896
Rocco Tozze	Rocky Kansas	Lightweight 1925–26
Louis Phall	Battling Siki	Light-heavy 1922–23
Francisco Guilledo	Pancho Villa	Flyweight 1923–25
John Cucoshay	Jack Sharkey	Heavyweight 1932–33
Barney Lebrovitz	Battling Levinsky	Light-heavy 1916–20
Ovila Chapdelaine	Jack Delaney	Light-heavy 1926–32
Eligio Sardinas	Kid Chocolate	Featherweight 1933
Vittorio Martino	Cannonball Martin	Bantamweight 1924–25
Gershon Mendelhoff	Ted 'Kid' Lewis	Welterweight 1915–16, 1917–19
Vincent Scheer	Mushy Callahan	Junior-welter 1926–30
Arnold Cream	Jersey Joe Walcott	Heavyweight 1951–52
Rocco Marchegian	Rocky Marciano	Heavyweight 1952–56

The name 'Rocky' has often been taken by boxers wishing to underline their toughness, and was used by Sylvester Stallone for his series of *Rocky* films. The first well-known fighter to adopt the name was Rocky Moore, who took the American middleweight title from George Rook in Boston in 1867.

Jack Johnson, who won the world heavyweight championship in 1908, was considered invincible and for a time leading contenders would not meet him. A tournament was held in California to discover the 'White Heavyweight Champion of the World'. In the final, a cowboy named Luke McCartney from Driftwood Creek in Nebraska knocked out Al Pazer in 18 rounds. McCartney was later killed in the ring when he fought Arthur Pelkey.

Johnny Coulon, world bantamweight champion from 1908 until 1914, went into vaudeville when he retired from his ring career. He had an unusual stage act. Although he seldom weighed more than 118 lb he would defy any member of the audience to lift him off his feet. Coulon would place a finger on the temple of the man crouching to lift him, disturbing the man's sense of balance.

In his European bouts, German-American heavyweight Ted Sandwina was managed by his mother, who claimed the title of The World's Strongest Woman.

In April 1888, Peter Jackson fought George Godfrey for what was billed as the 'Coloured Championship of the World'.

When the black American prize fighter Tom Molineaux first came to England he is recorded as having fought seven or eight 'unknowns' in different parts of the country. This is because white fighters did not wish to lose face by having it recorded that they had fought a black man.

In 1882 heavyweight champion John L Sullivan started touring the USA, boxing exhibition bouts with sparring partners. Spectators found these staged bouts dull. Then Sullivan had the idea of challenging anyone in the audience to last four rounds with him for a prize of $100. The innovation was wildly successful and the crowds flocked to see the Boston Strong Boy knock over a series of local inept hopefuls.

Tom Tring was footman to the Prince of Wales and moonlighted as a bare-knuckle fighter. Tring was beaten by Ben Brain in 19 minutes in 1789 at Dartford. The Prince, who had lost a great deal of money on the outcome of the fight, dismissed Tring on the spot.

Bare-knuckle fighter Ned Price was born of Quaker parents in England. He was well educated – some contemporary accounts state at Oxford – and continued

'Drink up, we're leaving!'

his boxing career in the USA. He worked as a court interpreter, qualified as a lawyer, became an actor-manager and wrote several successful plays for heavyweight champion John L Sullivan.

When Nino Valdez started to fight Joe McFadden at Sunnyside Gardens in New York there were less than 400 spectators in the arena. In the first round both boxers conducted such a battle that people watching the bout on television in adjacent bars rushed to the arena to buy tickets, doubling the crowd. Valdez stopped his opponent in the seventh round, after having been on the verge of defeat himself.

A pivotal plot development in Shakespeare's *As You Like It* is when the hero Orlando defeats Charles the Wrestler in a contest. However, when Australian boxer and trainer Larry Foley played the part of Charles in American star Louise Pomeroy's touring production of the play in Sydney, his combative instincts got the better of him. Foley knocked Orlando out, thus bringing the production to a premature end.

Many boxers have adopted nicknames but perhaps the most dramatic of them all was the one bestowed upon Stephen Oliver, a bare-knuckle fighter and protégé of champion Jack Broughton. Oliver's ring name was simply *Death*. He achieved this name not because he ever killed a man in the ring but simply because his complexion was so white.

World Boxing Association heavyweight champion Ernie Terrell played the guitar and sang with his group called the Heavyweights, which toured the USA.

Almost 30 years after Daniel Mendoza had toured England with his display, another British champion, Deaf Burke, decided to take a similar exhibition around the USA. In 1836, Burke, who had hurriedly left England after killing a man in a prize-fight, issued his bill of fare for American audiences:

The Champion Boxer of England, the Celebrated and Herculean DEAF BURKE
Mr Burke will make his first appearance as the Venetian statue, which he will exhibit on a pedestal, with appropriate change of figure, attitude, and expression. The arrangement is made in order to convey to the classical taste of artists, in an efficient manner, a series of beautiful compositions of ancient sculpture. The following is the order of the portraitures:

(1) Hercules, struggling with the Nemean lion, in five attitudes.
(2) Achilles throwing the discus or quoit, in two attitudes.
(3) The slave, Emoleur, the grinder, sharpening his knife whilst overhearing the conspirators.
(4) Two positions of the athletic combatants, as fighting gladiators.
(5) Samson slaying the Philistines with a jaw bone.
(6) The African alarmed at the thunder.
(7) Ajax defying the lightning.
(8) Romulus, from David's picture of the Sabines.
(9) Remus's defence from the same.
(10) Cain slaying his brother Abel.
(11) Samson lifting the gates of Gaza.
(12) The whole to conclude with the five celebrated positions of the dying gladiator.

Heavyweight John Harper from West Hartlepool so admired the American writer Jack London that he took the latter's name when he turned professional. As Jack London he won the British heavyweight title in 1944, losing it to Bruce Woodcock in 1945.

More films have been made about boxing than about any other sport. Among the biographies of champions which have been filmed are:

GENTLEMAN JIM (1942)

Errol Flynn plays the part of James J Corbett, the bank clerk who made gloved fighting a science and went on to take the heavyweight championship of the world from John L Sullivan. Sullivan is portrayed in a nice cameo role by Ward Bond, who went on to fame as the Wagonmaster in the television series *Wagon Train*. Playing one of Corbett's rivals is Jack Roper, who lasted all of a round with Joe Louis in 1939 and explained his lack of success against the champion by confessing, 'I zigged when I should have zagged!' It was Flynn's favourite film and is perhaps the best of all the boxing biopics, capturing the atmosphere of the sporting 1890s in a lush production.

THE GREAT JOHN L (1945)

Known in Britain as *A Man Called Sullivan*, this account of the rise and fall of the last bare-knuckle champion John L Sullivan is pretty turgid going. The star Greg McClure, in his first film, has a great physique but limited acting ability and his movie career petered out soon afterwards. There is one good scene, which never really happened, when Sullivan is kicked dizzy by a French *savate* exponent but manages to land one right hand which sends his opponent spinning like a top. The part of James J Corbett is played by Rory Calhoun, a former Golden Gloves participant. It looked as if Calhoun might go on to greater things than McClure, but his career dwindled away into 'B' Westerns.

THE JOE LOUIS STORY (1953)

This account of the life of the Brown Bomber ends with the veteran's crushing defeat at the hands of Rocky Marciano in 1951. Ironically the part of Louis is played by Coley Wallace, who defeated Marciano as an amateur. Wallace, who had a fair pro career, does not convince. A highlight of the film is a number of newsreel films of Louis's actual bouts spliced into the action.

SOMEBODY UP THERE LIKES ME (1955)

James Dean was scheduled to play the part of Rocky Graziano in this film of the unconventional middleweight's life and hard times, but was replaced after his fatal car crash by Paul Newman. Newman is far too handsome in the earlier scenes but marks up convincingly, thanks to the make-up artists. The fight scenes are realistic but, perhaps as a sop to the star, Newman is never shown losing a bout.

MONKEY ON MY BACK (1957)

Cameron Miller plays Barney Ross, the world welterweight champion and war hero who became dependent upon drugs after being treated for his war wounds and struggled to kick the habit. This is an excellent little film. Purists point out one flaw – a scene after Ross has lost his title shows the ex-champion's dressing room crowded with well-wishers. Cynics remarked that in reality there were no visitors after Ross had lost his title.

CITY OF BADMEN (1953)

The whole film is based around the world heavyweight championship bout between champion James J Corbett and challenger Bob Fitzsimmons at Carson City in 1897. This is an off-beat Western in which a gang of outlaws set out to steal the box-office takings. There are many cuts to the fight taking place, with stuntmen Gil Perkins

and John Day playing
Fitzsimmons and Corbett
respectively.

CHAMPAGNE CHARLIE (1944)

Tommy Trinder plays the lead in
this story of the 19th-century
music hall, but there is an
excellent cameo from Eddie
Phillips, former British light-
heavyweight champion, as Tom
Sayers, the bare-knuckle hero.

RAGING BULL (1980)

Voted the film of the decade, this
account of the life of former
middleweight champion Jake La
Motta owes much to the fine
central performance of Robert de
Niro, and more to the superb
direction of Martin Scorsese.
Between them they chart the rise
of the young Bronx fighter, his
troubled reign and his physical
deterioration. De Niro put on
50 lb in weight to aid his
performance as the overweight
nightclub comic which La Motta
became after his fighting days.
The fight sequences are
remarkably brief for a boxing
film.

Two other boxing films,
ostensibly works of fiction, were
based on the lives of real
champions.

THE GREAT WHITE HOPE (1970)

Although the protagonist, played
marvellously by James Earl Jones,
is called Jack Jefferson, the film is
based on the life of Jack Johnson,
the first black heavyweight
champion. We see Jefferson
reviled by whites who detest his
flashy lifestyle, finally agreeing to
take a dive against an inferior
white opponent. This is based on
the controversial ending to the
Jack Johnson–Jess Willard bout in
Havana in 1915, which Johnson
later claimed to have agreed to
lose.

THE HARDER THEY FALL (1956)

Humphrey Bogart, in his last film
role, plays a journalist who
becomes press agent for a huge
South American boxer, played by
wrestler Mike Lane, who is taken
over by mobsters and launched
on a series of fixed fights before
being abandoned without a cent.
The scenes of the opponents
making sure that they lose in a
number of spectacular ways are
very well done. The plot was
close enough to the life story of
Primo Carnera to encourage the
former heavyweight champion to
sue the makers.

Other successful boxing films
include:

BODY AND SOUL (1947)

Most people's favourite boxing
film. A gritty *film noire* in which
John Garfield fights his way from
the wrong side of the tracks to
the world championship but
loses his soul in the process. He is
redeemed after the death of his
sparring partner, played by
Canada Lee, a good welterweight
in real life. Garfield does not
throw the contest but puts his life
at risk by defying the gangsters
just before the last round and
knocking his opponent out. The
highlight of the film is the last
bout, photographed by James
Wong Howe, who moved about
the ring on roller-skates to get
close to the participants.

THE SET UP (1948)

Robert Ryan, former
heavyweight champion of
Dartmouth College, gives the
performance of his career as the
washed-out boxer whose backers
have agreed that he should take a
dive but have not bothered to tell
him, so convinced are they that
he will lose anyway. The action
of the film occupies the exact 72-
minutes running time, and is set
mainly in the dressing-room of a

sleazy boxing hall. The portrayals of boxers, handlers, hangers-on and spectators are beautifully done. In a tremendous fight climax Ryan defeats his opponent but is then beaten up by the enraged mobsters.

CHAMPION (1949)
Kirk Douglas gives a performance that made him a star, as the ambitious, heartless boxer who rides roughshod over everyone in his rise to the top but is finally killed in the ring. A good commercial Hollywood film with an impressive montage sequence as Kirk Douglas goes through his training routine which transforms him from a novice to a professional fighter.

FAT CITY (1972)
Director John Huston, a former professional boxer who once engaged in a memorable brawl with Errol Flynn at a Hollywood party, turns this film into a superb depiction of small-time boxers winning and losing. Stacy Keach is the veteran on the way out, while Jeff Bridges depicts a young hopeful who is never going to make it. Former professional 'Golden Boy' Art Aragon has a small role in the movie.

THE IRON MAN (1951)
Jeff Chandler plays the part of a heavyweight who develops a bad reputation but redeems himself when defending his title against challenger Rock Hudson. As a part of the publicity build-up for the film, Chandler boxed a public exhibition with heavyweight champion Jersey Joe Walcott.

KID GALAHAD (1937)
Wayne Morris became a mini-star in the role of a young bellhop with a hard punch who takes to the ring, but he is outpointed easily by supporting stars Humphrey Bogart, Edward G Robinson and Bette Davis. The film was remade with a paunchy and unconvincing Elvis Presley playing the boxer in 1962.

REQUIEM FOR A HEAVYWEIGHT (1962)
Anthony Quinn gives his all as a retired boxer forced to eke out a living as a professional wrestler, aided by manager Mickey Rooney. A television version in Great Britain set Sean Connery on the road to riches.

ROCKY (1976)
The first and best of the series, with Sylvester Stallone writing the script and playing the lead, but not directing on this occasion. One of the most financially successful of all boxing movies, it was based on Chuck Wepner's brave but unavailing battle against Muhammad Ali in which the underdog Wepner actually floored the champion, although Ali always claimed that he slipped! *Rocky* won Oscars for Best Direction and Best Editing.

Less successful – and deservedly so – were:

THE LEATHER SAINT (1955)
Handsome John Derek plays a parish priest who fights under an assumed name to earn enough money to equip a hospital. A poor film, it earned the scorn of boxing purists by showing the minister training on the day of a fight.

THE FLESH AND THE FURY (1952)
Tony Curtis plays a deaf-mute boxer who recovers his hearing but loses it again by insisting on fighting for the championship, when a blow to the head deafens him once more. A happy ending is ensured when Curtis hears people shouting about his victory as his hearing returns.

THE BIG PUNCH (1948)
A non-singing Gordon Macrae
refuses to throw a fight and has
to leave the big city to avoid the
vengeance of mobsters. He is
befriended by Wayne Morris, a
football player who has become a
priest.

WHIPLASH (1949)
Dane Clark becomes a prize-
fighter, although he would rather
be an artist. He falls into the
clutches of Zachary Scott, an
unlikely former boxer who is
now a crippled manager, and
falls for his wife, Alexis Smith.

THE GREATEST (1977)
Muhammad Ali certainly was a
great boxer, but only a so-so
actor, as this attempt to depict his
life shows.

Film star George Raft came out of
Hell's Kitchen in New York and
tried many routes to affluence.
He even had 17 professional
fights, being knocked out in
seven of them. In his last bout,
against Frankie Jerome, he
received 22 stitches to a wound
on his face and five dollars as his
purse. He spent the five dollars
on a pool cue and became a
professional hustler before taking
to dancing and then stardom in
movies.

THE DAY JOB

Tom Johnson won the bare-knuckle championship of Britain in 1789, after a period of 'crosses' and fixed fights had brought the ring into disrepute. His honesty brought credibility back to prize-fighting. Johnson had been a corn porter at the Old Swan Wharf, London Bridge. He was so strong that when a friend fell ill Johnson did the stricken man's work as well as his own, handing over the extra wage to the man's wife at the end of the week.

Isaac Perrins was 39 years old when he lasted 62 rounds with Tom Johnson for the bare-knuckle championship. He retired from the ring to become a publican. In December 1780 he rescued three people from a burning building, but caught pneumonia in the process and later died.

William Thompson, who fought under the name of Bendigo, served 28 terms of imprisonment for various offences, as well as winning the British bare-knuckle championship. He retired in 1851 and became an evangelist.

When Private Ham of the 9th Lancers was beaten in the finals of the Army middleweight championships in the 1890s, he claimed that the three-round distance had been too short for him to do himself justice. He challenged his conqueror, guardsman Sergeant Collins, to a return match over a longer spell.

The proposal attracted a great deal of interest. The two men were matched at the prestigious National Sporting Club in London, over ten rounds. Ham proved himself to have been right by outpointing the sergeant.

Former bare-knuckle champion Jem Mace toured the world with his boxing booth. On one occasion he put on a special display in the Australian outback for Ned Kelly and his gang of outlaws.

Snowy Baker of Australia won a silver medal at the 1908 Olympics. He went to California and earned a living teaching Hollywood stars to ride horses for their roles in films.

Former world featherweight champion Jim Driscoll was a sergeant-major Physical Training Instructor in the First World War. One of his sergeants was Johnny Basham, British and European welterweight and middleweight champion. Driscoll had Basham jailed for smoking while on duty.

In January 1914, Bill Ladbury of Deptford was outpointed by Percy Jones of the Rhondda Valley for the world flyweight championship. Both men then enlisted in the army. Ladbury was killed by a shell in France in 1917. Jones was gassed and lost a leg in the same conflict, dying of his wounds in 1922.

In 1915, veteran Scottish fighter Tancy Lee pulled off a major coup by stopping the great flyweight Jimmy Wilde in 17 rounds. In the small hours of the morning Lee and his followers arrived back at Leith and paraded loudly through the streets. 'Our Tancy has knocked out Jimmy Wilde!' they proclaimed. A woman threw up her bedroom window and snapped, 'They should both be out in France, knocking out the Germans!' The celebrations came to an abrupt end.

OCCUPATIONS OF WORLD HEAVYWEIGHT CHAMPIONS BEFORE THEY WON THE TITLE

John L Sullivan	Apprentice plumber
James J Corbett	Bank clerk
Bob Fitzsimmons	Blacksmith
James J Jeffries	Boilermaker
Tommy Burns	Semi-professional ice-hockey player
Jack Johnson	Wharf labourer
Jess Willard	Cowboy
Jack Dempsey	Labourer
Gene Tunney	Shipping clerk
Jack Sharkey	Sailor
Primo Carnera	Circus strong man
Max Baer	Cattle ranch worker
James J Braddock	Unemployed labourer
Joe Louis	Car factory labourer
Ezzard Charles	Soldier, World War II
Joe Walcott	Factory labourer
Rocky Marciano	Shoe factory worker
Floyd Patterson	Hotel handyman
Ingemar Johansson	Stone setter's assistant
Sonny Liston	Union enforcer, convict
Muhammad Ali	High school student
Joe Frazier	Slaughterhouse worker
George Foreman	Job Corps apprentice
Leon Spinks	US Marine
Larry Holmes	Sparring partner
Michael Spinks	Factory cleaner
Mike Tyson	Approved-school inmate

Guardsman Shaw, a veteran bare-knuckle prize fighter, lost his life at the Battle of Waterloo.

Tom Kennedy, an American heavyweight, was billed as the millionaire boxer.

Fidel La Barba won a gold medal in the flyweight class at the 1924 Olympics in Paris, and three years later won the world professional title. He then retired and became a student at Stanford University. Later he returned to the ring, but then settled for a career as a writer. He wrote the story from which the film *Footlight Serenade* was based. In the film Victor Mature portrayed a boxer who secured a part in a Broadway musical.

King Levinsky was apprenticed to a jeweller when he was a young man. It was a function of his job to deliver gems around Philadelphia. He was so frightened of the revolver he had to carry as protection that he learnt to box, so that he could defend his precious stones with his fists. He later became light-heavyweight champion of the world.

Paul Gallico was a prominent American sports writer who boxed at college and even sparred with Jack Dempsey in a training session. Towards the end of his career he decided that boxing was a barbarous sport, and wrote, 'If I were a dictator, I would abolish prize-fighting in my country by decree. I would scrap all rings, burn all boxing gloves and never let a youth be taught to strike another with his fist. For prize-fighting and boxing are stupid, senseless, unappetising, inefficient and one hundred percent useless!'

RHS Clouston, heavyweight blue and captain of boxing at Oxford University, turned professional in 1936 – with little success.

Freddie 'Red' Cochrane had the distinction of holding the world welterweight championship for 4½ years, yet lost the title the first time he defended it. Cochrane won the title from Fritzie Zivic in July 1941. The new champion then joined the forces and served in World War II. Consequently his championship was 'frozen' by the authorities. In February 1946, Cochrane made his first defence of the title. He was knocked out in four rounds by Marty Servo.

German Max Schmeling won the European heavyweight title in 1939. He was forced to give up the championship because of wounds received while fighting as a paratrooper in Crete.

Barney Ross became a professional fighter after gunmen murdered his grocer father in Chicago. He won and lost the world welterweight title. In 1938 he enlisted in the US Army. He was decorated for bravery and wounded on Guadalcanal. Treated with drugs for his injuries he became addicted and had a long battle before he finally kicked the habit.

Freddie Mills was one of the bravest of all British champions, but even he found service life tough. While serving with the RAF he went absent without leave.

Glen Moody, the Welsh middleweight champion, fought at Dunkirk while serving in the Army. During the retreat he encountered Ronnie James, British lightweight champion, who had been stranded with no boots. Moody carried James and his pack on his back until they encountered transport.

Lew Jenkins served in the Coast Guard in Sicily, Salerno, Normandy and Burma, after losing his world lightweight title in 1941. In 1951, serving as a master sergeant in the US Army in the Korean campaign, he was awarded the Silver Star.

Eddie Taylor, a light-heavyweight from Detroit, weighed in at noon at the Arena Gardens in his home city and then went home to rest before his scheduled match with Charley Taylor in January 1946. He did not turn up for the bout, which had to be cancelled and the ticket money returned to patrons. Later it transpired that Taylor had left home for the arena, but that on his way he had passed a small church called the Bethlehem

Temple. Overcome by an urge for peace Taylor had joined the congregation and renounced his boxing ambitions. 'I am now a man of peace,' he told reporters.

In 1947 and 1948, Jersey Joe Walcott gave heavyweight champion Joe Louis two sterling tussles for the latter's title. These were not the first encounters between the two men. Ten years earlier, while Louis had been training for his contest against Germany's Max Schmeling, Walcott had been hired as one of Louis's sparring partners. He was dismissed after two days' work, during which time he had floored Louis three times.

Joe Frazier broke his thumb winning the Olympic heavyweight final and returned home unable to turn professional. Appeals were made in local newspapers and over radio stations. Money was sent in and Frazier was given a job as janitor of the local Baptist church. It was a year before his thumb healed and he could turn professional. He went on to win the world championship.

East End gangsters Ron and Reggie Kray boxed as amateurs and professionals. Reggie reached the finals of the British schoolboy championships.

An actor called Harry H Harris III achieved considerable television exposure by portraying a boxer entering the ring in a

popular commercial for Budweiser beer. Harris became so identified with the sporting role that he had the bright idea of cashing in on his fame by turning professional. In his first bout he actually beat Ricky 'Junkyard Dog' Randall in 1983.

Irishman Terrie Christie, one of three graduate brothers, won both the Irish and French amateur titles in the same season and then turned professional in the USA, after qualifying as a doctor. He was leaving the ring after a bout in Lowell, Massachusetts in 1986, when the promoter's father had a heart attack at the ringside. Christie, still in his boxing gear, attended the stricken man before going back to the dressing room.

Sir Roy Welenski became Prime Minister of the Central African Federation. One of 13 children, he left school at the age of 14 to embark upon a number of different jobs. He won the amateur heavyweight championship of both Northern and Southern Rhodesia before entering politics.

World featherweight champion Willy Pep served in both the US Navy and Army in World War II.

John Ebenezer Samuel de Graft-Hayward was the son of a German father and West African mother. He won the amateur welterweight championship of the Gold Coast in 1935, and the middleweight championship of West Africa in 1941. After the war he turned professional, fighting under the name of 'The Chocolate Kid'. When Ghana became independent in 1957 he became a Lieutenant Colonel in its army. He transferred to the air force and was promoted to Air Commodore.

Former world light-heavyweight champion John Conteh did not have much luck with the restaurant he opened in 1980. It was called 'JC'. The theme was that of the former champion's initials. There were portraits of Julius Caesar, Julie Christie, Jaffa Cakes etc. In 1981, Conteh was fined £100 for throwing one of his waiters across several tables. Later in the year the business closed down.

One of the first converts to the Salvation Army in the 19th century was a prize-fighter called Peter Monk. He often acted as a bodyguard to General William Booth, founder of the movement.

Film star Mickey Rourke made his name by playing tough guys in such movies as *Wild Orchid*. In 1991, claiming that he was not being offered good scripts, he made his debut as a professional boxer at Fort Lauderdale, Florida, winning a four round decision over light-heavyweight Steve 'the Hammer' Powell, a garage mechanic. Onlookers were not impressed with Rourke's stumbling performance as he mugged and wrestled his way to

'Pleasant journey, Mr Dempster?'

a dull victory. The referee's post-match summary was caustic: 'It was Ringling Brothers . . . Barnum and Bailey. The other guy couldn't do anything . . . and he wasn't supposed to. And Rourke couldn't throw a punch.' The film star threatened to keep on with his new career until better roles turned up.

Scottish middleweight Bushman Dempster drove a log-cutting machine for a living. On one occasion he was driving his machine to Leith, where he was due to box, when his vehicle broke down. Dempster changed into his boxing kit and ran 15 miles to the hall, where he won a 15-round contest on points.

Elusive European middleweight champion Herol 'Bomber' Graham would appear in working men's clubs on stage with his hands behind his back, challenging anyone in the audience to land a solid punch on him.

American President Teddy Roosevelt was an enthusiastic boxer. He often sparred in the White House with former middleweight champion Mike Donovan.

Kid Wedge had over 70 professional contests; then at the age of 40 he entered academic life. He studied at the University of Arizona, became a minister of religion and professor of biology at Pasadena College.

'Two-Ton' Tony Galento got his nickname not for his considerable excess of weight but because he turned up late for a fight one night at a small hall, with this apology: 'Sorry, I had two tons of ice to deliver before I could get here!'

Before the First World War a young amateur boxer called Matt Wells had a good job making coins at the Royal Mint. One evening he sustained a cauliflower ear while boxing in a tournament at the German Gymnasium. When this was spotted at work he was given the sack at once. He turned professional. Later he won the world welterweight championship.

At least two famous footballers were the sons of professional boxers. Sir Stanley Matthews, outside-right for England, was the son of Jackie Matthews, protagonist of hundreds of fights in and around the Midlands. Dave Sexton, footballer and manager, was the son of Archie Sexton who fought Jock McAvoy unsuccessfully for the British middleweight championship.

Sam Collyer was born in England in 1842 but went to the USA as a boy. He fought in the Union Army in the American Civil War and won the Congressional Medal of Honor, the highest US award for gallantry. In 1866 he defeated Barney Aaron in 47 rounds at Pohick Landing for the lightweight championship of America.

Ben Hogan, a claimant for the bare-knuckle heavyweight championship of America in 1872 when he said that he had been robbed of the decision in his match with Tom Allen, was at different times a spy on both the Confederate and Union sides in the American Civil War, a gambler, and the inventor of the floating river gambling house.

After a prize-fight between Paddington Jones and Isaac Bilton in 1801, a drunken butcher called Berks reeled forward and challenged champion Jem Belcher, who was in the crowd. Belcher shrugged off his coat and came forward to give the upstart a thrashing for his impertinence. The butcher was defeated but put up such a good show that he was matched on two other occasions with the champion, losing narrowly each time.

Thomas Assheton-Smith, a well-known amateur boxer, stood as a candidate for Nottingham in a General Election towards the end of the 19th century. When he was heckled at one public meeting Assheton-Smith strode to the edge of the platform and declared, 'Gentlemen, as you refuse to hear the exposition of my political principles, at least be so kind as to listen to these few words: I will fight any man, little or big, directly I leave the hustings and will have a round with him now for love.'

THE HORIZONTAL
HEAVYWEIGHTS

The first contest with gloves for the heavyweight championship of the world was held between John L Sullivan, the bare-knuckle champion, and his challenger, the former bank clerk Gentlemen Jim Corbett. The bout took place at New Orleans on 7 September 1892. Corbett won on a knockout in the 21st round.

In the hundred years that followed, only one British heavyweight has won the world title. Bob Fitzsimmons was born at Helston in Cornwall in 1863. Unfortunately for national pride he emigrated with his parents to New Zealand when he was only nine years old. Later he became a naturalised American citizen.

It was claimed that Fitzsimmons was the ugliest of all the heavyweight champions. The possessor of a well-developed upper body, his legs were thin and spindly. He would pad his tights with cotton wool to add contours to his calf muscles. In addition to being knock-kneed and flat-footed, Fitzsimmons was covered in freckles and was bald apart from a few tufts of ginger hair, from which he derived his nickname of Ruby Robert.

However, Fitzsimmons was a master boxer with a devastating punch and the ability to withstand heavy punishment. He was the first man to win three world titles at different weights – the middleweight championship in 1891, the heavyweight crown in 1897, and the light-heavyweight title in 1903 at the advanced age of 41. Fitzsimmons never scaled much above 170 lb, although he once defeated Ed Dunkhorst, 'the Human Freight Car', who tipped the scales at 300 lb.

Fitzsimmons defended his title against James J Jeffries and lost it in 11 rounds in 1899 on Coney Island. Before a return contest, which he also lost, he made up a song, to the tune of Arthur Sullivan's *Tit Willow*, and delivered it to an audience at Begen Beach, Brooklyn:

> *By the shores of dear Begen,*
> *Lives honest old Fitz,*
> *With his wallop, his wallop, his*
> *   wallop.*
> *He met Gustave Ruhlin*
> *And knocked him out cold,*
> *With his wallop, his wallop, his*
> *   wallop.*
> *Then he took on Tom Sharkey*
> *And gave him a cramp,*
> *And he'll make big Jim Jeffries*
> *Look just like a tramp,*
> *And win back his title*
> *Of heavyweight champ,*
> *With his wallop, his wallop, his*
> *   wallop.*

Fitzsimmons had his last contest in 1914, at the age of 52, after a ring career of some 34 years.

He died of influenza in Chicago in 1917.

Fitzsimmons once came close to defeat against Peter Maher, an Irish heavyweight, at a bout held at the Olympic Club in New Orleans. Maher floored Fitzsimmons in the second round and it looked as if he would never beat the count, so his veteran second Joe Choynski reached over the timekeeper's shoulder and rang the bell, with over a minute of the round to go. By the time the confusion had been sorted out, Fitzsimmons had recovered. He went on to knock Maher out in the 12th round.

By trade Fitzsimmons was a blacksmith. On the road with his touring show he would sometimes present fans with horseshoes he had made. It was one of his favourite tricks to invite a supporter to pick up a horseshoe from the ground. The fan would then discover that the metal was still red hot.

Fitzsimmons first made his mark as a young man when former world champion Jem Mace promoted a tournament for lightweights at Timaru in New Zealand. Fitzsimmons knocked out four men to win the competition, only to be told that the gold watch intended for the winner had been left at home by Mace.

Disaster struck Fitzsimmons in the USA when he fought an exhibition with sparring partner Con Riordan. Riordan collapsed after the bout in 1894 and died in Syracuse. Fitzsimmons was tried for manslaughter and acquitted.

Eventually Fitzsimmons secured a bout with James J Corbett for the latter's heavyweight title. The two men ran into one another in a Philadelphia hotel in August 1895, before their bout. Corbett tweaked Fitzsimmons' nose and insulted him. The two men had to be separated.

When Fitzsimmons and Corbett met for the championship in Carson, Nevada in 1895, Fitzsimmons' second wife Rose, a trapeze artist, was present at the fight. When Fitzsimmons was getting badly beaten she screamed, 'Hit him in the slats, Bob!' Her husband took her advice, switched his attack to the body and won the championship with a 14th-round knockout.

At the height of his fame Fitzsimmons kept a pet lion with which he used to wrestle. When the beast died Fitzsimmons had it stuffed.

The first Briton to fight a world heavyweight champion with the gloves was Joe Collins from Leicester, who boxed under the name of Tug Wilson. In 1882 he met the champion John L Sullivan at Madison Square Garden. The bout was only over four rounds, but in the unlikely event of Wilson knocking Sullivan out he could have claimed the title. Such an eventuality was far from the Leicester man's mind. In order to make the match more attractive and even matters up a little, Sullivan offered his opponent $1000 and a share of the gate

Fitzsimmons the lion-tamer

Apart from Bob Fitzsimmons, 13 British heavyweights have fought a holder of the world heavyweight championship in gloved bouts, although not all of them have been recognised as championship bouts. Some of the earlier ones were officially classed as 'exhibitions'.

1882	Tug Collins	lost to	John L Sullivan	4 rounds	New York
1883	Charlie Mitchell	lost to	John L Sullivan	3 rounds	New York
1894	Charlie Mitchell	lost to	James J Corbett	3 rounds	Jacksonville
1883	Alf Greenfield	lost to	John L Sullivan	2 rounds	New York
1907	Gunner Moir	lost to	Tommy Burns	10 rounds	London
1908	Jack Palmer	lost to	Tommy Burns	4 rounds	London
1908	Jewey Smith	lost to	Tommy Burns	5 rounds	Paris
1909	Victor McLaglen	no dec.	Jack Johnson	6 rounds	Vancouver
1937	Tommy Farr	lost to	Joe Louis	15 rounds	New York
1955	Don Cockell	lost to	Rocky Marciano	9 rounds	San Francisco
1959	Brian London	lost to	Floyd Patterson	11 rounds	Indianapolis
1966	Henry Cooper	lost to	Muhammad Ali	6 rounds	London
1966	Brian London	lost to	Muhammad Ali	3 rounds	London
1973	Joe Bugner	lost to	Muhammad Ali	12 rounds	Las Vegas
1975	Joe Bugner	lost to	Muhammad Ali	15 rounds	Kuala Lumpur
1976	Richard Dunn	lost to	Muhammad Ali	5 rounds	Munich
1986	Frank Bruno	lost to	Tim Witherspoon	11 rounds	London
1989	Frank Bruno	lost to	Mike Tyson	5 rounds	Las Vegas

The record of British heavyweights in international competition is so dire that in the 1920s an American sports writer dubbed them the Horizontal Heavyweights, and the term has stuck.

receipts if he was still on his feet at the end of the four rounds. Wilson won the money by the ignominious ploy of falling down and taking a count of nine every time he was struck. In the opening round he went down nine times, and when he was not on the canvas Wilson was either embracing his opponent ferociously or else scuttling backwards around the ring like a petrified crab. In the second round Wilson did a little better and only went down eight times before the booing crowd. In the third round the Englishman varied his tactics and stayed upright, clinching and running, but still paying four long visits to the canvas. Sullivan chased his elusive opponent in disgust, swinging wild punches. When the final bell went Wilson cheerfully collected his $1000 and returned to Leicester. The authorities refused him a licence to open a public house because his character was not good enough. Instead Wilson bought a shoe shop with his winnings and retired from combat, if indeed he had ever been in it.

Another British challenger, perky Charlie Mitchell from Birmingham, had slightly better fortune against John L Sullivan in their gloved contests. He actually floored Sullivan in the first round of their 1883 bout in New York. The affronted champion got to his feet and administered a sound thrashing to the Englishman before the police stopped the contest in the third round. The two men were matched again, but Sullivan turned up drunk and the bout was cancelled.

None of John L Sullivan's British challengers had much luck against the Boston Strong Boy. Alf Greenfield of Birmingham was stopped by the champion in two rounds at Madison Square Garden in 1884. Afterwards both men were arrested and hauled before the court, accused of participating in an illegal prize-fight. Greenfield conducted himself with great dignity in the witness box. 'We hired the hall through our managers,' he declared self-righteously. 'It was just to make a little money. I had no ill-feeling and he had no ill-feeling. We do it in England all the time.' The all-male jury was out for a perfunctory eight minutes before returning with a verdict of Not Guilty.

It was not only the American heavyweights who bowled over their English counterparts. The reputation of the horizontal heavyweights spread so rapidly that big men from all over the world were eager to pick up easy money against the British champion. In 1889, Australian Frank Slavin was matched in a bare-knuckle bout with British champion Jem Smith at Bruges in Belgium. Slavin thrashed the Englishman mercilessly for round after round, until Smith's supporters invaded the ring to prevent their man being knocked out. The intimidated referee declared the bout to be a draw, prompting Slavin to protest, 'I have come sixteen thousand miles to win; why the blazes can't you give a man a chance?'

Tommy Burns, the world heavyweight champion, had the foresight to come to England for some easy pickings in 1907 and 1908. He knocked out Gunner Moir, the British champion, in ten rounds and then co-promoted a bout against Jack Palmer in London. To show that he was no mug, Burns had all the locks on the stadium changed, so that his partners could not sneak anyone in without his knowledge. Burns then sat in the box office counting heads as the patrons came in, and made sure that all the takings were locked up. Only then did he go and change into his boxing gear, stroll down to the ring and knock Palmer out in four rounds.

Another glove fighter to make an early visit to England was black heavyweight Sam Langford. He knocked out two English heavyweights in 1907 and then returned to knock out the British

'THIS is my referee!'

champion Iron Hague in four rounds in 1909. Langford had the practice of allowing his opponents to look good for a few rounds, until his manager had the opportunity to place a few bets on his man. As soon as Langford received the signal he would then move in and dispatch his opponent with ease. During the preliminary discussions for the bout with Iron Hague, Langford was asked for his choice as referee. The fighter had smiled lazily and displayed an enormous fist. 'This is my referee,' he drawled.

Bombardier Billy Wells, British heavyweight champion, was a great favourite with fans just before World War I, bowling over most home-grown opponents with ease. Wells seldom enjoyed good fortune against overseas opponents. In 1912 he visited the USA, where he was matched against several leading American heavyweights. He scrambled a win against Tom Kennedy, but in his bout with Al Pazer, Wells knocked his opponent down for a long count but then walked into a similar punch himself and lost all interest in the proceedings.

English heavyweights were considered such easy pickings that when Eddy McGoorty came over from the USA to fight British big man Frank Goddard in 1920, in the early hours of the morning of the fight he was discovered drunk and incapable in the streets of London. Later that morning he was fined at a magistrate's court, and that evening he went in against the hard-punching Goddard still suffering from a hangover. Goddard knocked him out.

Phil Scott was the British heavyweight champion from 1926 until his retirement in 1931. On his visits to the USA he was regarded as almost the prototype of the horizontal heavyweight. He had a custom of clutching his groin and sinking dramatically to the canvas, with a feeble cry of 'Foul!' For this habit he was dubbed by American newsmen variously as Phoul Scott and Phainting Phil. In the course of a few years he won on disqualifications against such opponents as George Cook, Armand de Coralis, Ricardo Bertazollo, Yale Okun, Ted Sandwina, and Otto von Porat. In the bout against von Porat in New York in 1929, former champion Jack Dempsey was the referee. In the second round Scott performed his customary folding-up act, protesting that von Porat had hit him below the belt. Dempsey, who had never claimed a foul in his life, pleaded with the Englishman to continue. Obdurately Scott refused to rise. With great reluctance Dempsey disqualified von Porat, after a few well-chosen words had been directed at the recumbent Englishman. The victory over von Porat qualified Phil Scott for a championship eliminating bout with American Jack Sharkey. In the third round Sharkey probably did hit Scott low, but by this time American audiences and referees were fed up with Phainting Phil's antics, and as Scott squirmed elaborately on the floor of the ring, the referee coldly counted

him out. Scott had two more contests, lost them both and retired from the ring.

One of the better British big men was Welsh heavyweight Tommy Farr, who went 15 rounds with world champion Joe Louis in 1937. Perhaps Farr should have quit while he was still ahead. He remained in the USA for a number of contests and lost them all – against Jim Braddock, Max Baer, Lou Nova and Red Burman.

Immediately after the Second World War Britain had a promising heavyweight champion in Bruce Woodcock, who had little trouble from European opposition. However, he did not usually do too well against American imports. Tami Mauriello knocked him out and Joe Baksi broke his jaw. Woodcock defeated Gus Lesnevich, a light-heavyweight, and Lee Oma, a former convict who did not come to fight. He also secured a win over Lee Savold on a disqualification but was stopped in a return bout recognised in Great Britain, but nowhere else, as being for the world championship.

Don Cockell was a promising light-heavyweight who suffered from a glandular condition which caused him to become grossly overweight. He won the British heavyweight title and rather foolishly challenged Rocky Marciano for the world title. Cockell fought bravely in their 1955 San Francisco bout, but the odds were stacked against him. To aid the heavy-punching, all-action Marciano, the ring size was reduced from 20 ft to 16½ ft. Instead of the 6 oz gloves agreed upon, heavier 8 oz gloves were used. The referee turned a blind eye to the champion's rough-house tactics. One experienced observer reckoned that Cockell was struck low three times and after the bell on four occasions, while Marciano also employed a variety of head butts, kidney punches and various other infringements. The referee stopped the bout in the champion's favour in the ninth round. Before the bout Cockell had stated that if necessary he would match Marciano foul punch for foul punch during their bout. Afterwards he was asked why he had not adhered to this game plan. Cockell shook his head. 'I had to think about foul punches, and that took too long,' he said. 'With Rocky they came naturally!'

American heavyweights continued to knock over British opposition in the 1950s and 1960s but British fighters encountered peril from another direction – Sweden. Ingemar Johansson had been disqualified for not trying in the finals of the 1952 Olympics in Helsinki, but as a professional no one could accuse him of not doing his best, especially against English big men. In succession he flattened Joe Bygraves, Peter Bates, Henry Cooper, Joe Erskine, Dick Richardson and Brian London, although the latter floored Johansson with the final punch of their bout in Stockholm

in 1963. Johansson was saved by the bell and given the points decision. He then retired.

The inimitable Muhammad Ali knocked out most of his opponents in his heyday, and his British opponents were no exception. Joe Bugner went the distance with him twice, in 1973 and 1975, but his detractors reckoned that in the second of their bouts, at least, the Hungarian-born British boxer was more intent on going the distance than actually trying to win. Otherwise Ali stopped Henry Cooper twice, although he was famously floored in their first bout, and also won inside the distance against Brian London and Richard Dunn.

In the 1980s, popular British heavyweight Frank Bruno was brought along on a series of carefully-selected opponents. When he stepped up a class or two he was not so successful. Two Americans, Bonecrusher Smith and Tim Witherspoon, both stopped Bruno, who later went on to lose in five rounds to Mike Tyson. A few years later, when Tyson was asked whether he thought it was a good idea for Bruno to be making a come-back, he replied, 'Sure, there's nothing American heavyweights like better than beating up on good old Frank Bruno!'

PUBLIC RELATIONS

An early history of bare-knuckle pugilism in song was composed and sung by actor John Emery in the 19th century. The verses dealt with most of the early champions of the prize-ring.

Come listen, all ye fighting gills
And coves of boxing note, sirs,
Whilst I relate some bloody mills
In our time have been fought, sirs.
Whoe'er saw Ben and Tom display,
Could tell a pretty story,
The billing-bout they got that day,
Send both ding-dong to glory.
    Singing fal la la, etc.

Now Ben he left it in his will
As all his pals declare it,
That who the hero's chair would fill
Must win it or not wear it;
No tainted miller he could stand,
Right sound must be his cat's-meat,
Who could not bear his hide well
    tanned
Was quite unfit for that seat.

All nations came to claim the prize,
Amongst them many a don, sirs,
And Bill Ward swore, b–t his eyes,
He'd mill 'em everyone, sirs,
At Bexley Heath, it hapt one day,
He was beaten black and blue, sirs,
By one deep in the Fancy lay,
'Twas little Dan, the Jew, sirs.

The Ruffian, Young, next on the list,
Laid claim to boxing merits,
A mere pretender to the fist,
Who dwelt in wine and spirits.
His hits were RUM none could
    deny,
His blackstrap none could bear it,
But of his hogshead he was shy,
Lest they should tap his claret.

Bitton then came, a champion bold,
And dealt some hard and sly knocks,
But when all the truth is told
Some rank him with the shy cocks;
But prate like this we must not
    mind,

A Dutchman true begot him,
Whoe'er has seen Bitton behind
Will ne'er dispute his bottom.

Of all the milling coves the crack,
None pleases more than Sam, sirs,
Whose whiskers are of jetty black,
As those of whip, Jeram, sirs,
So neatly fibs the Israelite,
To every stander-by, sirs,
Who must allow it has a sight,
Worth well a Jew's eye, sirs.

We now must sing of Belcher's fame,
Whose race was full of glory;
His matchless deeds I need not name,
You all must know his story.
He beat the best coves of his day,
But few could stand before him,
For he could hit and get away,
If not – why, he could floor them.

Champion of the milling corps,
Next starts a true Game Chicken,
His honours to the last he bore,
But never bore a licking;
Till tyrant Death, man's greatest foe,
Who mercy shows him never,
Hit poor Pearce a mortal blow,
Which closed his eyes for ever.

Jack Gully made a manly stand
In science quite complete, sirs,
He rather chose to fight on land,
Than serve longer in the fleet, sirs.
Where many worthies of their line,
Like Jack for bravery noted,
Are under hatches left to pine,
Nor hopes to be promoted.

Next rings the fame of gallant Cribb,
A cool and steady miller,
Who late to Yorkshire went to fib
A first-rate man of colour.
No matter whether black or white,
No tint of skin could save him,
A horse's kick was pure delight,
To the belly punch he gave him.

England's champion now behold,
In him who fills the chair, sirs,
Who never yet a battle sold,

Nor lost one in despair, sirs,
For in each contest or set-to,
Brave Tom bore off the laurel,
Which proudly planted on his brow,
Says – 'Touch me at your peril.'

Now fill your glasses to the brim,
And honour well my toast, sirs,
'May we be found in fighting trim,
When Boney treads our coasts, sirs.'
The gallant Barclay shall lead on,
The Fancy lads adore him,
And Devil or Napoleon,
Leave us alone to floor him.

Muhammad Ali was not the first fighter to express himself in verse. Bare-knuckle contender Bob Gregson composed at least one poem. Entitled *British Lads and Black Millers* it dealt with the first contest between British champion Tom Cribb and his black American opponent Tom Molyneaux in 1810:

The garden of freedom is the British
*   land we live in,*
And welcomes every slave from his
*   banished land,*
Allows them to impose on a nation
*   good and generous,*
To incumber and pollute our native
*   soil,*
But John Bull cries out loud,
We're neither poor nor proud,
But open to all nations, let them
*   come from where they will.*
The British lads that's here,
Quite strangers are to fear,
Here's Tom Cribb, with bumper
*   round, for he can them mill.*

Tom Sayers was one of the smallest of British bare-knuckle fighters but secured a 42-round draw in his international contest with American John C Heenan in 1860, despite fighting with a badly damaged arm. Sayers' son later became a music hall artiste.

The highlight of his act was a song about his famous father's ring career:

My friends I now inform you,
I'm the son of the Tom Sayers,
Who fought fifteen great battles
In one and twenty years.
So grant me your attention,
And I'll attempt to show,
How my father did succeed
Great men to overflow.

So I'll leave the stage one second
And reappear to show
How my father used to stand,
And how he used to go.
The first he fought was Aby Crouch,
And beat him in twelve rounds
By his superior science then
For five and twenty rounds.
To fight with Young Dan Collins,
And at it they did go,
Then forty-four warm rounds they
*   fought*
And went just so.

In fifty-two he beat Jack Grant,
Round sixty, for a blow
Sent brave Jack to Mother Earth,
And proved his overthrow.
In fifty-three Jack Martin tried
To beat, but Tom said 'No',
For in the twenty-third hard round,
Down poor Jack did go.

Next he met Nat Langham,
And at it they went sweet,
And for the first and only time,
My father met defeat.
In fifty-four he beat George Sims,
And in fifty-five I'll show
How he beat Harry Paulson,
And went just so.

In fifty-seven he beat Aaron Jones,
Tipton Slasher and Brettle;
And in January fifty-eight
Floored Aaron like a skittle.
Next Paddock tried to take the belt,
But came to grief and woe,
Then he twice defeated Benjamin,
And went just so.

In sixty he met Heenan,
At Farnboro' toe to toe,
Each in turn his best did try

His man to overthrow.
The sporting world will not forget
That great event I know,
For just like lions both men fought
And went just so.

So, by way of finish, I must say
Since my father's grand farewell,
The noble art of self-defence
Into the shade hath fell,
Never more to rise again,
After standing many years,
Held up by pluck and fair play,
In the days of brave Tom Sayers.

So, friends, be generous in my cause,
My efforts crown with cheers,
And that will ever glad the heart
    of Young Tom Sayers.

One of the first patrons of pugilistic art was the retired prize-fighter Joe Ward. The walls of his Soho public house were filled with paintings of prize-fights, from the first champions to 1812.

John Gully, who fought his way out of a debtors' prison to the championship and became a millionaire Member of Parliament, is portrayed by Charles Dickens in *Nicholas Nickleby* as the boastful MP Mr Gregsbury.

When a young journalist called George Bernard Shaw saw British heavyweight Charlie Mitchell fight an exhibition, he was so impressed that he began to study the literature of the sport in the British Museum Library. In 1882, the 26-year-old Shaw published his second novel. It took for its theme professional prize-fighting and was entitled *Cashel Byron's*

Profession. The book told the story of a young public school boy who ran away to Australia and learnt to box in a Melbourne gymnasium. Cashel Byron went on to become a well known bare-knuckle champion and to win the hand of an aristocratic lady. The book was not a success and Shaw had to wait until he was over 40 before he discovered his true metier and achieved fame as a playwright, the author of such successes as *Major Barbara* and *Pygmalion*.

William Thompson, who fought as Bendigo, gave his name to a public house in Nottingham, a brew of beer, two races for horses and an Australian cathedral city, complete with its Bishop.

Jack Dempsey, former world welter and middleweight title holder, died in poverty in 1895. In 1899 an anonymous poem was published about his neglected grave in the *Portland Oregonian*. As a result of this, enough money was collected to erect a headstone, upon which this poem was engraved:

Far out in the wilds of Oregon,
On a lonely mountain side,
Where Columbia's mighty waters
Roll down to the ocean side;
Where the giant fir and cedar
Are imaged in the wave,
O'ergrown with firs and lichens,
I found Jack Dempsey's grave.

I found no marble monolith,
No broken shaft or stone,
Recording sixty victories,
This vanquished victor won;
No rose, no shamrock could I find,
No mortal here to tell
Where sleeps in this forsaken spot
Immortal Nonpareil.

A winding wooden canyon road
That mortals seldom tread,
Leads up this lonely mountain
To the desert of the dead.
And the Western sun was sinking
In Pacific's golden wave
And those solemn pines kept
watching,
Over poor Jack Dempsey's grave.

Forgotten by ten thousand throats,
That thundered his acclaim,
Forgotten by his friends and foes,
Who cheered his very name.
Oblivion wraps his faded form,
But ages hence shall save
The memory of that Irish lad
That fills poor Dempsey's grave.

Oh, Fame, why sleeps thy favoured
son
In wilds, in woods, in weeds,
And shall he ever thus sleep on,
Interred his valiant deeds.
'Tis strange New York should thus
forget
Its 'bravest of the brave'
And in the fields of Oregon,
Unmarked, leave Dempsey's grave.

Several decades later Dempsey's name was brought to public attention again when a young heavyweight called William Harrison Dempsey took the Christian name of 'Jack' and won the world heavyweight title in 1919.

Many heavyweight champions have had biographies written about them, but flamboyant and hard-drinking John L Sullivan, who lost the first heavyweight title fight with the gloves to James J Corbett in 1892, is the only one to have been the subject of a work of fiction. The novel was entitled *Congressman John L.* It was published soon after Sullivan's retirement from the ring, and the author's *nom-de-plume* was Argus. In the book Sullivan gives up drinking, is

elected to Congress and sets out upon a series of crusades to right wrongs. The former champion even joins the Salvation Army. He raises money for the poor and modestly refuses the offer of the Presidency of the USA, after surviving an assassination attempt on the floor of the House. When asked for his comments on the novel, Sullivan replied, 'The people could do far worse than send me as their representative to Congress.'

Inhabitants of Southampton were keen to know how their heavyweight Joe Beckett had fared against Frenchman Georges Carpentier in their 1919 encounter in London. It was arranged that as soon as the result was known, red rockets would be fired in the air if Beckett lost, and blue ones would be fired if he won. Minutes after the bout had started the air was full of red flashes. Beckett had lasted less than a round.

Beckett was a doughty but unskilled British heavyweight who seldom did well against overseas opponents. In an effort to improve his image, he purchased a mansion near Southampton and tried to set himself up as the local squire. Behind his back, irreverent fight fans referred to their champion as the Count of Ten.

Tiger Joe Fox was a very good black American light-heavyweight of the 1930s. In 1939 he disappointed his followers when he was stopped in a final eliminator for the world title in nine rounds. Fox hardly threw a punch throughout the contest, but he had reason to believe that the fates were against him. A month before the bout he had been stabbed in a Harlem hotel by a lady friend, losing a great deal of blood in the process. To make matters worse, just before his eliminator with Melio Bettina, the superstitious Fox read in the newspapers that his opponent had hired a hypnotist to put him under the influence. In turn the alarmed Fox hired Ben 'Evil Eye' Finkle as his own mesmerist to counter Bettina's Svengali. The fighter wore dark glasses at the weigh-in to ward off any malevolent glares. Later, when members of Bettina's entourage entered his dressing room to inspect his hand bandages, Fox covered his eyes with his hands to deflect any transmissions.

In a fit of boredom, American sports writer Elliott Harvith created a fictitious heavyweight called Bagelbag Nazerman and started writing about the fighter's exploits. These were taken so seriously that Harvith became alarmed and announced that Bagelbag had retired undefeated after 30 contests.

As a part of the publicity build-up for his challenge for Joe Louis's heavyweight title, 'Two-Ton' Tony Galento wrestled an octopus in a tank. The octopus later died.

No one could accuse Scottish promoter Nat Dresner of running down-market promotions in the

1920s. His Master of Ceremonies was Sir Iain Colquhoun, while the timekeeper was the Marquess of Clydesdale.

Rocky Graziano and Jake La Motta were two of the toughest and most extrovert middleweights of the 1940s and 1950s. Each had a ghosted best-selling autobiography, *Somebody Up There Likes Me* for Graziano and *Raging Bull* for La Motta, both of which were filmed. The two men never met in the ring, which was just as well for the nervous disposition of any referee appointed to the contest. Once, however, the two middleweights went on an all-night drinking session. They woke up on the sidewalk of an unfamiliar section of New York. Squinting at the sky, La Motta asked, 'Is that the sun or the moon up there?' 'I dunno,' grunted the equally hung-over Graziano. 'This ain't my neighbourhood!'

British welterweight John H Stracey, who defeated Jose Napoles for the world title in 1975, would present visiting cards upon which were inscribed *John H Stracey – Professional Pugilist*.

Muhammad Ali set the standard for showmanship in professional boxing. He admitted freely that he had taken the idea from a professional wrestler, Gorgeous George (George Wagner). George sold out the Olympic Stadium in Los Angeles on each of the 27 occasions that he appeared there. He would be preceded into the ring by a valet in morning dress, who would fumigate the ring and his master's opponent with a Flit gun containing a perfumed disinfectant. George would then enter the ring wearing a fur-trimmed robe. His long blond hair would be encased in a gold-spun hair-net. The wrestler made a point of sneering at any old ladies in the audience and informing hecklers that they were beneath his contempt. In the intervals between rounds he would primp his hair before a mirror held up by his valet. George was introduced as 'The Human Orchid'. He made one of the worst sports movies ever filmed. It was called *Alias the Champ* and was shot in two weeks.

In 1973, the BBC insisted that Italian bantamweight Franco Zurlo put tape over slogans on his shorts for an Italian hangover cure.

The first postage stamps depicting boxers were issued by the Greek government to mark the occasion of the 1896 Olympics. Among a number of sporting stamps there were two showing statues of ancient Greek boxers.

One of the great artists of the world of boxing in the literal sense was Sam Rabin, who painted many pictures of the boxing scene. He was selected to sculpt the marble memorial to Freddie Mills, after the light-heavyweight champion's

untimely death. Twice he won the first prize at the Biennale of Sport in Fine Art for his drawings. Under his real name of Rabinovitch he won a bronze medal for wrestling at the 1928 Olympics in Amsterdam. Later he boxed and wrestled professionally. He had a number of fights at the Blackfriars Ring, and wrestled as Rabin the Cat. He dabbled in acting, playing the part of the wrestler bested by Henry VIII, played by Charles Laughton, in *The Private Life of Henry VIII* (1933). He also played the Jewish prize-fighter Daniel Mendoza in *The Scarlet Pimpernel* (1934). One of Rabin's supporters in the ring was artist Augustus John, whose own son Edwin boxed as a professional middleweight. Sam Rabin died in 1991.

The British Boxing Board of Control would not allow American middleweight Iran Barkley into England to fight Nigel Benn because they said he suffered from an eye injury. Instead Benn fought Barkley in Las Vegas in 1990. After the contest, while being interviewed on television, Benn tore up his Board of Control licence in protest because he had not been allowed to fight Barkley in Britain. Benn had stopped Barkley in the first round.

The editor of the *San Francisco Bulletin* was so convinced that James J Jeffries would win his 1910 comeback bout against champion Jack Johnson that on the afternoon of the contest he issued an edition with the headline *Jeffries Knocks Out Jack*

'Hold that back page – and the rest of them!'

Johnson. When news came through over the telegraph that Johnson had stopped his white opponent the editor sent messengers round the city, buying back bundles of the newspaper at inflated prices, so that they could be pulped.

Jose Torres, former Olympic silver medallist and world professional light-heavyweight champion, has written biographies of Muhammad Ali and Mike Tyson, and is a close friend of famed author Norman Mailer.

A MATTER OF TIME

Charlie Davies was much too good for his opponent John McConnell when they fought for the British middleweight title in London in 1873. McConnell was floored many times, making the bout a travesty. The authorities introduced a new rule. In future any boxer knocked down would only have ten seconds in which to regain his feet. Should he be unable to do so he would be declared 'knocked out of time'. This was how the term 'knockout' entered the sport.

Al Singer did not expend a great deal of time and energy during his period as world lightweight champion. He won the title by knocking out Sammy Mandell in 1 minute 46 seconds in July 1930. Four months later he lost it to Tony Canzoneri – in 1 minute 6 seconds.

Johnny Buff left it late to start his boxing career. He did not turn professional until he was demobilised from the US Navy in 1918, when he was 30 years old. In 1921 he won the American flyweight title and then took the world bantamweight title from Pete Herman in New York in the same year. He was then 34 years old. Buff fought on for another five years and then re-enlisted in the Navy at the age of 38.

Sid Burn was a prominent East End boxer just before the First World War. During this period he employed a youthful sparring partner called Ted 'Kid' Lewis. He punished the younger boxer severely during their training sessions. Years later, after Lewis had matured and captured the world welterweight title, he in turn employed the now over-the-hill Burn as *his* sparring partner and returned the compliment.

Ironically, another young sparring partner, Roland Todd, learnt his craft from Lewis in the gymnasium and later took the latter's titles from him.

It is difficult to ascertain which boxer had the most contests over a fighting career. Some boxers 'inflate' their record or include exhibition matches or fights on boxing booths. In Great Britain the holder of the 'most confirmed genuine contests' record is Len Wickwar of Leicester, a featherweight. Between 1928 and 1947 Wickwar had 462 contests, of which he won 336.

In 1948 two leading contenders for the heavyweight title were matched at Madison Square Garden in a major event. Joe Baksi hurt his ankle in training and was unable to meet Gino Buonvino. Baksi's place was taken by washed-up heavyweight Lee Savold, who came out of semi-retirement for the occasion. Savold pulled off the upset of the year to knock Buonvino out in 54 seconds, a

His Grace as referee

record for Madison Square Garden. His win revitalised his career, even securing him a lucrative bout with Joe Louis. Four years later Joe Baksi eventually got his shot at Gino Buonvino. By now both fighters were well over the hill, and they met in a small hall in New York. Baksi won – in 54 seconds, the exact time it had taken Savold to floor Buonvino.

Manager Felix Bocchicchio managed to get his charge heavyweight Joe Walcott no fewer than five title attempts before Jersey Joe finally managed to win the championship. Walcott lost twice on points to Joe Louis, in 1947 and 1948, twice on points to Ezzard Charles, in 1949 and 1951, before he finally got lucky and knocked Charles out in seven rounds in Pittsburgh, also in 1951. Walcott lost his title to Rocky Marciano in 13 rounds in Philadelphia in 1952.

One of the first press accounts of boxing in Britain occurred in *The London Protestant Mercury* in January 1681: 'Yesterday a match of boxing was performed before his Grace the Duke of Albermarle, between his butler and his butcher. The latter won the prize, as he hath done many times before, being accounted, though but a little man, the best at that exercise in England.'

Mountainous George Foreman was 42 years old when he challenged Evander Holyfield before 19 000 spectators in Atlantic City in 1991. Former

champion Foreman put up a great fight before losing on points. He said that he had done it for all senior citizens everywhere.

Roberto Duran and Sugar Ray Leonard fought twice in 1980, each winning one bout for the world welterweight title. They had to wait nine years, until 1989, before they fought the rubber contest. This time Leonard defeated Duran for the world super-middleweight championship.

Heavyweight champion Jack Johnson defended his title against fellow black American Jim Johnson in France in 1913. In the eighth round Jack Johnson sustained a broken arm. The referee called the verdict a draw, although the bout should have been stopped in favour of Jim Johnson and the latter declared the new champion.

Dado Marino of Hawaii became the first grandfather to hold a world championship when he defeated Terry Allen for the flyweight title in 1950.

HP (Pat) Floyd was the most successful of all British amateur heavyweights. He won the ABA title three times and was finalist on four other occasions between the two world wars. During the Second World War Floyd served in the RAF Regiment and retired from the ring.

However, in 1946 a Frenchman called Mennegault was the clear favourite to win the amateur heavyweight championship of Great Britain. Newspaper writers persuaded Floyd to take off 42 lb in weight and enter the championships, at the age of 34. Reluctantly he did so, and outpointed Mennegault in the final to win the ABA championship for the fourth time at heavyweight.

In 1816, Jacob Hyer fought a grudge contest against Tom Beasley, won it and jocularly claimed the bare-knuckle championship of America, the first man to do so. Hyer then retired. Twenty-four years later his son Tom also claimed the title and defended it successfully on a number of occasions.

A glittering future was predicted for London middleweight George Davis, who defeated Freddie Mills twice, once on a knock-out just before World War II. Like many other boxers Davis joined the Army. He was killed in a tragic barrack-room accident when a rifle being cleaned by another soldier went off.

The first contest with gloves for the heavyweight championship of the world is generally held to be that between John L Sullivan, the bare-knuckle champion, and James J Corbett in New Orleans in 1892, when Corbett won in 21 rounds. However, a programme for 1885 stated that a bout between Sullivan and Dominick McCaffery at Chester Park, Cincinnati was to be 'six rounds to decide the Marquis of Queensberry glove contest for the

championship of the world'. The bout went the distance but then referee Billy Tait jumped out of the ring without announcing the decision and went to Toledo. Two days later someone reminded him that he had not declared the victor. 'Oh, Sullivan won,' he replied casually.

The referee could not decide between Australians Les Darcy and 'Guv'nor' Balsa after ten rounds at Thornton in 1910. He ordered the exhausted boxers to fight an extra round. Darcy won on points over the unusual 11 rounds distance.

A reluctant Sergeant J Gardner was ordered to make up the numbers at a Grenadier Guards boxing tournament held at Windsor in 1948. He stepped into the ring a complete novice and knocked the army heavyweight champion out in two rounds. Within four months Gardner had won the British amateur heavyweight title and went on to become the British professional heavyweight champion by defeating Bruce Woodcock.

Heavyweight Frank Goddard bore a grudge for six years against Bombardier Billy Wells. In 1916 Goddard acted as a sparring partner to Wells, then the British champion. When the training camp broke up, a punchball bladder belonging to Goddard was mistakenly packed among Wells's gear. Wells did not reply to Goddard's letter asking for the return of the bladder. Goddard took this as a personal slight. Six years later, in

In 1950 Associated Press published the results of its mid-century poll to ascertain the best pound-for-pound boxers of the first half of the century. They were:

1 .. Jack Dempsey .... heavyweight
2 .. Joe Louis .... heavyweight
3 .. Henry Armstrong .... featherweight, lightweight, welterweight
4 .. Gene Tunney .... heavyweight
5 .. Benny Leonard .... lightweight
6 .. Jack Johnson .... heavyweight
7 .. Jim Jeffries .... heavyweight

1922, he was matched against Wells at the Crystal Palace in London. Goddard told his friends that at last he was going to get his own back on Wells over the punchball incident. Goddard went on to beat Wells in six rounds, after a ferocious battle.

Walter McGowan reigned a long time as flyweight champion of Britain, but no local opponents of a high enough standard could be found to meet him. The British Boxing Board of Control accordingly waived its rule that a champion had to have three successful bouts for the title before becoming entitled to keep a Lonsdale Belt. The Board presented McGowan with a belt because there was no one good enough to fight him for it.

In October 1991, Mitch 'King Kong' Sammons knocked out Terry Anderson, thus scoring his 15th consecutive first round knockout win.

THEY NEVER COME BACK

It is an axiom of professional boxing that retired boxers can never make it back to the top again. Many have tried . . .

Jem Belcher was one of the lightest but bravest of the bare-knuckle champions. At the peak of his fame he lost an eye whilst playing rackets. He was only 21 and was playing with a well-known amateur, Edwin Stewart. The ball struck Belcher in the eye, and after several operations the eye had to be removed. Several years later, in 1805, he attempted a comeback but lost his unbeaten record, losing to Hen Pearce and twice to Tom Cribb.

After Daniel Mendoza had lost his bare-knuckle title to John Jackson in 1795, he retired for 11 years, opening a school of boxing and writing his memoirs. The lure of the ring was too strong and he essayed a comeback in 1806, defeating Harry Lee in 53 rounds. Mendoza then waited another 14 years and in 1820 lost to Tom Own in 12 rounds, at the age of 57.

In 1905, John L Sullivan was a fat and out-of-condition 46-year-old, weighing 273 lb. It had been 13 years since he had lost to Jim Corbett for the world title. That did not stop Sullivan making one last comeback. In Grand Rapids, Michigan he went in against 200 lb Jim McCormick, some twenty years his junior. Sullivan connected with a wild swing in the second round, knocking his opponent out. Sullivan at once challenged Bob Fitzsimmons and James J Jeffries, but settled for touring with McCormick, fighting a series of exhibition contests, which reinforced a suspicion that their first contest had been a put-up job to gain Sullivan one last series of pay-days.

Novelist Jack London was just one of the many newspaper writers who implored retired heavyweight champion James J Jeffries to leave his alfalfa farm and meet the unpopular black champion Jack Johnson. The badly-advised Jeffries did just that. He took off more than 30 lb in order to win the offered £40 000 at the age of 36, after an absence of six years from competitive boxing. He was thrashed and stopped in the 15th round by Johnson in Reno, Nevada in 1910, the first and last defeat of his career.

Jim Driscoll of Wales was the British and European featherweight champion. When he met Abe Attell in America he took every round, according to spectators, in his 'no-decision' contest with the world champion. Driscoll retired in 1913, but came back six years later at the age of 39 and met French boxer Charles Ledoux at the National Sporting Club. Driscoll outboxed his opponent with ease for the first 14 rounds, but was stopped in the

16th. Before he left the club the members had raised a subscription of several thousand pounds for his retirement.

Tommy Burns held the world heavyweight championship between 1906 and 1908, before retiring to become a manager and promoter. When he visited England in 1920 at the age of 39, he thought so little of the British heavyweight champion Joe Beckett that he challenged him. The match was made and Burns boxed well for several rounds before he was stopped by the much younger British fighter in the seventh.

Many followers of boxing consider Benny Leonard to have been the finest boxer of all time. He held the world lightweight title from 1917 until 1924. He retired a wealthy man but lost most of his money on the stock market. He made a comeback after seven years in retirement, and from 1931 onwards won 19 fights, although he was 35 years old. Then Leonard was matched with Jimmy McLarnin, who knocked him out in six rounds. Leonard retired again, this time for good.

Jack Dempsey, former world heavyweight champion, retired in 1927 after his second unsuccessful contest with Gene Tunney for the title. In 1931, he attempted a comeback, fighting as many as five opponents in a single night, up and down the country, in a so-called series of exhibition matches. Dempsey did so well in these bouts that unwisely he decided to test himself against a rated heavyweight, Kingfish Levinsky, in Chicago in 1932. Dempsey could not get near the smart and cautious younger man, and after a few more bouts his comeback petered out.

Joe Louis retired in 1950. Many consider him to have been the greatest of all the heavyweight champions. A year after his retirement, plagued by debt and tax demands, he tried a comeback, fighting Ezzard Charles, the new heavyweight champion, in New York. Charles easily outpointed a man he had once idolised. Louis plodded on for a few more bouts and then went into permanent retirement after he had been knocked out in eight rounds by Rocky Marciano in 1951, when he proved to be a shell of his former fighting self.

Tommy Farr, against whom Joe Louis had made the first defence of his championship, made his comeback the year before Joe Louis went into permanent retirement. Former British heavyweight champion Farr had retired in 1940. Ten years later, at the age of 36, he attempted a comeback. He had 15 fights in three years and lost only four of them. He even regained the Welsh heavyweight title, which he had first won in 1936. In the end Farr was stopped in eight rounds by Don Cockell in 1953, and hung up his gloves again.

Larry Holmes had once been Muhammad Ali's sparring partner when Ali was the world heavyweight champion. By 1980

Holmes was the title-holder and 38-year-old Ali had been in retirement for two years when he challenged Holmes and they met in Las Vegas. Ali looked in good shape, but he had taken off too much weight too quickly, and he was as weak as a kitten. He hardly threw a worthwhile punch at his opponent. Holmes begged the referee to stop the contest, but the official would not do so. Ali did not come out for the 11th round. A year later Ali lost to Trevor Berbick in Nassau and retired for good.

Eight years after Larry Holmes had punished former champion Muhammad Ali, the positions were reversed. Now Holmes, an ex-champion, was challenging the new king, Mike Tyson. Holmes came out of retirement to meet Tyson in Atlantic City. The once great Holmes did not have a chance. He was knocked out in four rounds.

George Foreman had won the world heavyweight championship in 1973 and retired soon after losing the title to Muhammad Ali in Zaire in 1974. Foreman became a minister of religion and developed an appetite for junk food, increasing his weight to 18 stone. In 1987, at the age of 37, he started a comeback, rattling off a series of victories against second-raters. When Foreman was matched with Evander Holyfield for the world heavyweight championship everyone expected the old man to fold up after a round or two. Instead, although being well beaten, 42-year-old Foreman put up stubborn resistance and went the distance. He was still boxing and winning in 1992.

ALL SHAPES AND SIZES

Gentleman John Jackson, prize-fighting champion of Great Britain in 1795, was also an accomplished sprinter and long jumper. He could lift a 1000 lb weight from the ground, and write his name on a wall above his head while suspending an 84 lb weight from his little finger. He became a boxing instructor to the nobility and numbered the poet Lord Byron among his pupils.

When Gentleman John fell and broke his leg in the fourth round of his fight with George Inglestone in 1789, he offered to fight on if both of them would agree to be tied to chairs with their arms free. Inglestone had the sense to refuse the offer and was declared the winner.

Irish bare-knuckle fighter Simon Byrne punished Sandy McKay so severely that the latter died after their contest in 1830. Byrne was tried for manslaughter but acquitted. The Town Crier of Stony Stratford, McKay's home town, composed the epitaph engraved on the dead man's tomb:

Strong and athletic was my frame,
Far from my native home I came,
And manly fought with Simon
*   Byrne,*
Alas, but lived not to return.
Reader, take warning by my fate,
Or you may rue your case too late;
If you have ever fought before
Determine now to fight no more.

Three years later Simon Byrne fought James Deaf Burke near Ascot racecourse. Byrne collapsed and died after the fight, which lasted 99 rounds.

Irish bare-knuckle champion Dan Donnelly claimed to have been knighted by the Prince Regent (later George IV), and was often refereed to as 'Sir' Dan Donnelly. After his death, the fighter's body was exhumed by bodysnatchers. For many years the mummified remains of what was said to be Donnelly's right arm was displayed in a public house near Kilcullen.

'Iron Man' Joe Grimm weighed in at 144 lb in 1905 when he fought future heavyweight champion Jack Johnson, weighing 220 lb. Grimm was knocked down many times but he lasted the full six rounds against one of the most fearsome punchers of all the champions.

Jess Willard was the tallest man to win the world heavyweight title, being over 6ft 6in tall. The gigantic cowboy did not turn professional until he was 28 years old and lost his first bout as a professional, having never fought as an amateur. He went on to take the title from Jack Johnson in Havana, Cuba on a 26-round knockout in 1915, when Willard was 32.

Despite the severity of many of the bare-knuckle contests, many of the old time champions lived to a good old age, as may be seen from this chart. Some were not so lucky:

Year Won Title		Age at Death
1719	James Figg	39
1734	George Taylor	44
1740	Jack Broughton	86
1750	Jack Slack	58
1760	Bill Stevens	42
1771	Peter Corcoran	30
1783	Tom Johnson	47
1791	Ben Brain	41
1794	Daniel Mendoza	83
1795	John Jackson	76
1800	Jem Belcher	29
1803	Hen Pearce	32
1807	John Gully	80
1808	Tom Cribb	68
1821	Tom Spring	57
1824	Tom Cannon	69
1825	Jem Ward	84
1827	Peter Crawley	65
1833	James Burke	36
1840	Nick Ward	39
1841	Ben Gaunt	46
1845	Bendigo	69
1850	William Perry	61
1851	Harry Broome	39
1856	Tom Paddock	39
1857	Tom Sayers	38
1861	Jem Mace	80
1863	Tom King	53
1869	Mike McCoole	49
1873	Tom Allen	63
1876	Joe Goss	57
1880	Paddy Ryan	48
1882	John L Sullivan	59

When Frank Moran, an American heavyweight, surveyed his opponent, lanky British champion Bombardier Billy Wells, he remarked with satisfaction, 'He's all chin from the waist up!' Moran knocked Wells out in ten rounds in their 1915 bout.

Heavyweight contender Jack Bloomfield confirmed his promise when he knocked out Bombardier Billy Wells in 1922. When Bloomfield tried to lift the unconscious Wells to drag him back to his corner he sustained a hernia which effectively finished his boxing career.

'Professor' AJ Newton, ABA lightweight champion in 1888 and 1890, became a well-known trainer at his Islington gymnasium. After his death his training duties were taken over by his son Andy, with considerable success. Andy Newton was blind.

After Billy Papke lost to Stan Ketchel in 1909 in a 'grudge fight', Papke was so badly mauled about the face that his own sister could not recognise him after the contest.

In 1887, American Jack McAuliffe was not doing very well against English import Jem Carney in their world lightweight title fight with bare knuckles. In an effort to get Carney disqualified, McAuliffe's second, Jack Dempsey, a former lightweight

champion himself, bit his man on the shoulder until the blood flowed. McAuliffe rushed out at Carney and suddenly shouted 'Look at the blood! He's biting me!' Carney opened his mouth to protest and revealed that he had no teeth.

London policeman Harry Mallin was a strong favourite to win the middleweight gold medal for the second time at the 1920 Olympics in London, but was outpointed by the Frenchman Brousse. When Mallin got back to his dressing room Brousse's teeth-marks were noticed on the policeman's shoulder. The Frenchman was disqualified and Mallin went on to win the gold medal again.

The 1915 battle in Brooklyn between Battling Levinsky and Sandy Ferguson was a fierce one. Levinsky won on points but Ferguson bit him so many times that the winner needed 20 stitches in his wounds afterwards. The Commissioners suspended Ferguson for life, but later reduced the period to six months. For the rest of his ring career Ferguson would be heckled with cries of 'Had your lunch yet, Sandy?'

The longest career of any professional boxer in Great Britain was probably that of West Indian Sam Minto, who fought all over the world between 1910 and 1938. Born in 1883, he also had hundreds of contests on the boxing booths. Bob Hartley, who toured the country with Minto, said, 'At practically every town we visited there would be someone Sam had fought during his ring career and who was prepared to pick up a few pounds by boxing him again on the booth.'

The kidney punch was banned after two particularly vicious bouts involving its use, on opposite sides of the world. When Ben Jordan fought Harry Greenfield of Camden Town at the National Sporting Club in 1899, he knocked his opponent out in the ninth round with a punch to the kidneys which caused the loser so much obvious distress that the club declared that particular blow to be illegal. At about the same time George Dawson fought Jem Burge in Australia and spent most of the bout hitting Burge in the kidneys, which were an obvious target because of the latter's boxing stance. Burge collapsed after the bout and the kidney punch was also banned in Australia.

When American flyweight Frankie Genaro arrived in Britain to defend his world title against Johnny Hill in 1929, he was greeted with the news that Hill had collapsed and died. Instead of going into training Genaro went straight to Strathmiglo for the Scot's funeral.

When aspiring young light-heavyweight Gene Tunney returned from service with the Marines in World War I, he discovered that his left arm was suffering from a wasting disease and was withering away. Doctors told him to forget his ambition of following a career as a professional boxer. Tunney ignored them and went to work as a lumberjack in the woods of Maine. He spent months chopping trees and sawing wood, using his left hand as much as he could. When he returned to New York, a potent left jab was one of the deadliest weapons in the armoury which took him to two victories over Jack Dempsey and the heavyweight crown.

In September 1928, the Illinois Boxing Commission decreed that in future two stretchers must be positioned at the ringside to carry away any boxers knocked unconscious in the ring. It was expressly forbidden for seconds to toss senseless fighters over their shoulders and carry them through the crowd into the dressing room.

As a young man, Paul Berlenbach, future world light-heavyweight champion, was deaf and dumb. One day he climbed a telegraph pole and received a shock from a loose cable. His speech and hearing returned.

Len Johnson was a noted middleweight of the 1930s. He defeated such British and European champions as Len Harvey, Gypsy Daniels and Ted 'Kid' Lewis. Yet Johnson was never allowed to fight for a British title. Johnson was black, and coloured boxers were not allowed to fight for British championships until after World War II.

'Where's your gumshield, George?'

After a few particularly gory bouts in the 1940s, the New York Athletic Commission decreed that boxers should not wear white shorts, as these tended to show up the blood being shed in the ring. It was ordered that fighters should wear black or deep purple trunks only. So many boxers ignored the edict that it was never enforced.

Two novice British heavyweights, Jim Moran and George Nuttall, met in 1951. Moran hit Nuttall so hard that his opponent swallowed his gum shield. The bout was stopped in Moran's favour. Nuttall was reported to be extremely choked.

Former ABA light-heavyweight champion and professional prospect Nicky Piper of Cardiff has such a high IQ that he is a member of Mensa, the society for gifted people.

On 8 January 1947, world featherweight champion Willie Pep was one of the survivors of a plane crash in New Jersey. He sustained a broken back and leg, and was in a body cast for five months. He was told that his boxing days were over. In June of the same year, a month after having the cast removed, Pep outpointed Victor Flores over ten rounds at Hartford. He went on to take part in more than 150 more contests before retiring in 1966.

Floyd Patterson and Ingemar Johansson had three epic fights for the world heavyweight title between 1959 and 1961. Patterson won two out of the three bouts. When both men retired Patterson still showed his supremacy. He finished ahead of Johansson in the New York Marathon.

Max Baer, former world heavyweight champion, had a way with words until the end. When he suffered a heart attack in a New York hotel he staggered to a telephone and asked for a doctor. 'A house doctor?' asked the receptionist. 'No, dummy,' whispered the stricken Baer, 'a people doctor.'

World heavyweight champion Joe Louis punched so hard that his manager found it difficult to recruit sparring partners for the Brown Bomber. While Louis was preparing for a contest with Max Baer, his manager commissioned a saddle-maker to create a leather body protector for the use of the hired help getting into the ring with the young contender.

Britain's Don Cockell was a promising young light-heavyweight when something went wrong with his metabolism. Suddenly everything he ate or drank seemed to turn to fat. His weight ballooned from 12½ stone to almost 15 stone. Undeterred, Cockell continued boxing as a heavyweight and did well enough to fight Rocky Marciano for the world championship.

In 1965, Booths Gin sponsored a £2000 competition to find a promising heavyweight boxer. One entrant, an 18-stone giant called Pat Roach, was fancied to do well, but he was not allowed to compete because he refused to shave off his beard. Roach went on to become a very popular wrestler and the star of a number of successful television series, including *Auf Wiedersehen, Pet* and *Scott of the Antarctic*.

Heavyweight David Bey had a successful amateur career despite the fact that he weighed a substantial 294 lb. When he turned professional he was ordered to reduce his weight to a svelte 220 lb before he could be considered suitable for substantial television exposure.

Craig Bodzianowski, an American cruiserweight, had 13 successful professional contests before losing a leg in a motorcycle accident. He continued his fighting career with an artificial limb, and three years later, in 1987, he was outpointed by Alfonzo Ratcliff in a bid for the WBC world title.

On 2 November 1985, former lightweight contender Kenny Lane lost an eight-round points decision to 25-year-old Dave Guerra at Grand Rapids, Michigan. Lane was 53 years old.

After a lengthy lay-off due to a torn retina, Britain's popular heavyweight Frank Bruno arrived at the British Boxing Board of Control's offices in 1991 to argue his case for the return of his licence. Arriving with Bruno in his chauffeur-driven Mercedes to reinforce his case were his solicitor, barrister and trainer. Bruno promptly led them all to the wrong entrance and had to be re-directed to the correct door.

Scientific tests showed that Bruno's punch was the equivalent of being hit with a padded 12 lb sledgehammer travelling at 20mph.

James 'Bonecrusher' Smith, the only graduate to win a version of the world heavyweight crown, had a 1983 fight at Ridgewood Grove called off when he could not fit his huge hands into any of the gloves provided.

American light-middleweight Tyrone Trice claimed that he felt strangely tired during his bout with Argentinian Julio Cesar Vasquez in Paris, in September 1991. Trice was stopped in nine rounds. After the bout he discovered that the gloves he had been given weighed 10oz, compared to the normal 8oz pair worn by his opponent. Trice went to the offices of the French Boxing Commission to complain but could find no one there who spoke English.

French featherweight Eugene Criqui had part of his jaw blown away in World War I and had a piece of bone grafted on to it to make a new chin. It was claimed that this made it almost impossible to knock him out. In any event Criqui went on to win the world title from Johnny Kilbane in 1923.

Belfast promoter Barney Eastwood could not find enough local fighters to head his bills at the Union Hall. He began to import fighters from Central and South America. Many of them took up residence in Belfast. Among the boxers entering the country were champions from Panama, Venezuela, Puerto Rico and many other Hispanic countries.

Australian aborigine Dave Sands became a leading contender for the world middleweight championship before he was killed in a road accident in 1952, just before he was due to box Randolph Turpin for the vacant title. In addition to the Empire middleweight championship he won the Australian heavyweight, light-heavyweight and middleweight championships. He was one of six boxing brothers – Dave, Russell, Alfie, George, Clem and Ritchie. Between them they took part in 494 professional bouts.

THEY FOUGHT
THE LAW

Jem Belcher was one of the greatest of the 19th-century bare-knuckle fighters, but also one of the unluckiest. He lost the sight of one eye playing rackets and then was knocked out after 40 minutes in 1809 by Tom Cribb. Belcher spent 28 days in prison for taking part in this illegal prize-fight, where he caught a severe cold. This developed into TB and Belcher died in 1811 at the age of 29.

Australian Les Darcy was such a popular young middleweight in New South Wales that when he lost one of his early contests his enraged supporters burnt the hall down.

In 1882, Mr Justice Hawkins handed down a celebrated decision which declared prize-fighting to be illegal:

'Every fight in which the object and intent of each of the combatants is to subdue the other by violent blows is a breach of the peace; and it matters not in my opinion whether such a fight be a hostile fight begun in anger, or a prize fight for money or other advantage. In each case the object is the same, and in each case some amount of personal injury to one or both of the combatants is a probable consequence; and although a prize fight may not commence in anger, it is unquestionably calculated to rouse the angry feelings of both before its conclusion. I have no doubt then, that every such fight is illegal and the parties to it may be prosecuted for assaults upon each other. Many authorities support this view.'

One of the most controversial title-fight decisions of the modern era was delivered at Madison Square Garden in New York in July 1952. The Cuban Kid Gavilan outpointed the classy American welterweight Billy Graham over 15 rounds. There were rumours of a 'fixed' fight, reinforced years later by an alleged death-bed confession from one of the judges of the bout. Four years later Gavilan, now an ex-champion, was on the receiving end of a similar decision when he was adjudged to have lost on points to British welterweight Peter Waterman in London in 1956. The referee had his licence taken away after this bout.

One of the worst referees in the history of the sport was Maxie Moore, who flourished in the USA towards the end of the 19th century. The nadir of Moore's career was reached at Coney Island in August 1894. Jack McAuliffe, the world lightweight champion, was undefeated in almost 50 contests but was approaching the end of his career. He was matched against the mercurial Australian Young Griffo, one of the most brilliant boxers of his time. However, Griffo could usually be relied upon the enter the ring in an advanced state of intoxication.

Against McAuliffe, to the chagrin of many gamblers and supporters of the champion, Griffo entered the ring in a sober state. He proceeded to hand out a boxing lesson to the Irish-born McAuliffe. At the end of 10 one-sided rounds Moore was on hand to protect the champion's record by declaring McAuliffe to be the winner on points, to the fury of the crowd but to the great relief of the champion's camp. The verdict was considered so diabolical that for years in boxing circles a dubious decision was henceforth referred to as 'a Maxie Moore'.

Stanley Ketchel was one of the gamest of all American middleweights. In 1910 he was shot and killed by a farm hand jealous of the attention Ketchel was paying to his girlfriend. The sporting world mourned the loss of a great champion. Writer Wilson Mizner, when informed of Ketchel's death, said simply, 'Start counting – he'll get up at nine!'

When Jackie Brown won the British flyweight title by knocking out Bert Kirby in three rounds at West Bromwich in 1929, it was the first time that a British championship bout had been held on a Sunday.

In a bout held in South Africa one Saturday night, Australian Max Gornick fought 14 hard rounds with South African Charlie Smith. The clock struck midnight. A lawyer in the crowd pointed out that if the bout went into the 15th round it would be taking place on Sunday and thus breaching the Sunday Observance Act. The contest was declared a 14-round draw.

After the first black heavyweight champion Jack Johnson had defeated former champion Jim Jeffries in ten rounds in 1910, there were racial disturbances all over the USA. The following day the death toll was given as: New York 1, Uvaldia 3, Little Rock 2, Houston 1, Omaha 1, Mounds 1, Tyler 1. Total 10. The film of the fight was banned in many cities and severely cut in many others to avoid scenes of Jeffries being hurt.

Teddy Baldock of Poplar defeated former world flyweight champion Emile Pladner of France on a sixth-round foul in 1930. Promoter Jeff Dickson accused the fighter of 'acting'. Baldock sued for libel and won the case, gaining costs and an apology.

Henry Armstrong lost his world lightweight championship to Lou Ambers on points over 15 rounds in New York in 1939. His chances were not helped by the fact that five of the rounds were taken away from him for hitting below the belt.

Bermondsey Billy Wells was once matched against world welterweight champion Micky

Walker in Chicago. At a meeting before the bout Wells was introduced to gangster Al Capone. No one knows what took place at the meeting, but Wells did not turn up for the 1926 contest and it had to be cancelled.

Kid McCoy, former light-heavyweight champion of the world and inventor of the 'corkscrew' punch, was arrested in 1924 for the murder of his girlfriend and the shooting of three other people. The 56-year-old former champion pleaded 'guilty but insane' and was sentenced to a long term of imprisonment. When he was released he committed suicide in a Chicago slum in 1940.

Del Fontaine was a Canadian middleweight who fought the best American and British middleweights and welterweights, including world champion Micky Walker. One day Fontaine pursued his girlfriend, a young dancer called Hilda Meek, into the street and shot her dead. He was found guilty at the Old Bailey of murder and sentenced to death. He was hanged on 29 October 1935.

Jim Elliott had an eventful life. Born in Ireland in 1838, he went to the USA and took up a career as a bare-knuckle fighter. In 1863 he lost on a foul to Jim Dunne, and shortly afterwards served his first term of imprisonment, two years for theft. He came out of jail and resumed his fighting career. In 1867 he won the American heavyweight championship by knocking out Bill Davies in nine

rounds at Point Pelée Island, Lake Erie, Canada.

Three years later Elliott was sentenced to 16 years' imprisonment for highway robbery, assault and battery with intent to kill. The champion had mugged a well-known minstrel singer, Hugh Dougherty, beating him viciously. In prison Elliott underwent an eye operation, which reduced his powers of sight considerably. He evidently did not serve his full term of imprisonment, because by 1879 he was fighting again, the only trade he knew.

In 1882 he was knocked out in three rounds by the up-and-coming John L Sullivan. Sullivan magnanimously threw $50 on top of Elliott's prostrate form. Elliott drifted back into a life of crime but was so hard up that he was matched with Sullivan again. Before the bout could take place Elliott was shot and killed by a gambler in a Chicago saloon.

Tongan Kit Lave met most of the best British heavyweights in the 1950s. When he found contests hard to come by, he challenged any boxer to meet him in a contest with bare fists. He was severely reprimanded by the British Boxing Board of Control.

In 1991, the House of Lords defeated by a tiny margin a proposal to make professional boxing illegal.

Even if he managed to turn up sober, alcoholic Young Griffo would drink bottles of beer between the rounds of his contests. Finally, when a New

'I could do with a drink'

York judge sentenced him to three days in gaol for being drunk and disorderly, Griffo went berserk and attacked the judge. The boxer was committed to an asylum for two years. Although he lost only nine of 166 bouts, he died in poverty in New York in 1927.

When Cleveland 'Big Cat' Williams fought Muhammad Ali for the latter's world heavyweight title in 1966, he was almost literally a shadow of his former self. Williams had been renowned as one of the strongest men in the heavyweight division until, in 1964, he had an altercation with a Highway Patrol officer who accused the boxer of drunken driving. In the course of the dispute the policeman shot Williams with a .357 Magnum. Williams almost died, losing 50 pounds in weight. Slowly he built his physique back up again, but he was no longer the threat he once had been. Ali stopped the Big Cat with ease in three rounds.

In 1967 Rubin Carter, former middleweight contender, and his sparring partner John Artis were convicted for the shotgun slaying of three people in a New Jersey bar, allegedly as a reprisal for the killing of a black man. Carter always protested his innocence strongly. While he was in Trenton, New Jersey maximum security prison he wrote a book about his experiences, *The 16th Round*. Many celebrities took up the boxer's cause, and Bob Dylan wrote a song called *Hurricane* about Carter. Eventually the New Jersey Supreme Court ordered a new trial and Carter was released on bail. He was convicted for a

second time and remained in jail for another eight years. He was freed in 1985, after a US district court ruled that Carter and Artis had been denied their proper civil rights. In 1988 it was announced that there would not be a third trial.

Leon Spinks' tenure of the world heavyweight championship was short-lived. He won it from Muhammad Ali and then lost it back to him in 1978. Spinks became better-known for the fact that his minder was the actor 'Mr T' who later starred in the television series *The A Team* and the film *Rocky 3*. Mr T became Spinks' minder as a result of winning a television competition. He was probably a better actor than a bodyguard, because on one occasion Spinks was so badly mugged that he even lost his gold tooth.

A would-be hold-up man entered a Pittsburgh store in 1983 and demanded money from the proprietor and a 72-year-old customer. The elderly patron promptly floored the intruder and roughed him up. The terrified robber fled, leaving behind his wallet and sweat-shirt. The pensioner who had engaged him was Billy Conn, former world light-heavyweight champion and twice challenger for Joe Louis' heavyweight crown.

Donnie Hood defeated Dave Buxton in five rounds in 1991. The venue of the bout was an unusual one – Shotts maximum security prison in Scotland.

The gloves don't pass mustard . . .

Jack Bonner was falling behind in his 1899 bout with leading middleweight Tommy West when Bonner's seconds smeared their man's gloves with oil of mustard. West was blinded by the acrid solution and stumbled back, complaining to the referee. The referee growled, 'I can smell it!' and disqualified Bonner.

Several Tunisian boxers lost their licences in 1950 when they were discovered taking part in an illegal tournament near Casablanca. The boxers concerned were blindfolded and were fighting with lumps of wood strapped to their hands.

In December 1952 at Madison Square Garden, Joe Giardello defeated Billy Graham on a split decision. One judge voted for Graham, while the referee and the other judge voted for Giardello, who was declared the winner. It was an unpopular decision. Members of the New York Boxing Commission took the scorecard of the judge who had voted for Giardello and changed his points, making Graham the winner. The commissioners announced that Graham was now the winner. They said that there had been rumours of a betting coup and they were not satisfied with the scoring of one judge. The whole affair went to court and it was decided that the commissioners had no right to interfere with the scores of any judges, the original verdict must stand, and Giardello was still the winner.

Ali Lukusa of Zaire did not do very well in his bout against Frank Bruno at the West Berlin Sportshalle in 1982. After being knocked out in two rounds he went for a walk and was mugged and beaten up by four men.

The World Boxing Council deprived Marvin Hagler of his middleweight title for fighting too long at Las Vegas in 1983. Hagler defeated Roberto Duran over 15 rounds, while WBC rules stipulated that no championship contest should last longer than 12 rounds.

William Thompson of Nottingham fought under the ring name of Bendigo. He was one of the smartest fighters to win the bare-knuckle title. His brother John, a prosperous optician, deplored William's illegal prize-fighting activities and would often inform the authorities before Bendigo fought, causing the bouts to be cancelled. In the end John provided William with a pension of a pound a week, as long as he kept away from the ring.

Dick Turpin outpointed Vince Hawkins over 15 rounds at the Aston Villa football ground in 1948. Turpin was the first black man to be allowed to fight for a British title by the Board of Control, and the first black champion under its auspices.

After 14 exciting rounds Matt Wells was disqualified at the Blackfriars Ring against Australian Hughie Mehegan. The crowd went wild. Someone tried to set fire to the press box and a ringsider produced a gun and went after the referee. The man was disarmed and the revolver was later given to the referee as a souvenir.

The stuffy members of the National Sporting Club, which claimed the right to organise British championship contests in the opening decades of the 20th century, were horrified when they heard that the British welterweight title was being fought for in Australia in 1914. The champion Johnny Summers had journeyed to the Antipodes and agreed to defend his championship there against Tom McCormick. McCormick won and claimed the title, although the NSC refused to countenance his claim. To make matters worse, Matt Wells also went to Australia, where he beat McCormick, and claimed the title in turn. Things were not sorted out until Johnny Basham beat Summers, McCormick and Wells in England and was regarded as the official champion.

English lightweight Johnny Summers pulled off a great upset when he knocked out leading American Jimmy Britt in the open air at Canning Town in 1909. Unfortunately the tournament became famous not for the boxing taking place, but because it was the scene of the greatest organised gathering of pick-pockets ever known at a public exhibition in modern times. The thieves got away with thousands of pounds. Towards the end of the jamboree they were openly mugging spectators at the ringside.

Lightweights in the ring, light fingers at ringside

Future world lightweight champion Benny Leonard had his first recorded fight when he was selected to represent his New York street gang against the best fighter of the Sixth Street gang, to settle a territorial dispute. The fight was held on a vacant lot and Leonard won in four rounds.

The early history of American boxing is reflected in the laws passed to legislate it in and around New York. Between 1896 and 1900 boxing contests were sanctioned under the Horton Law. This was followed by the Lewis Law from 1900 until 1911, which barred boxing in public but allowed contests to take place in clubs. From 1911 until 1917 the Frawley Law allowed public contests as long as they did not exceed ten rounds and no decision was given. After three years of confusion the Walker Law was adopted in 1920, legalising boxing in New York. This led to boxing becoming lawful all over the USA.

In the 1920s, boxing administrators began to get worried about the number of bouts ending in fouls. The states of Oklahoma and Missouri declared that any bout ending in a disqualification should be refought on another occasion, with the boxers concerned fighting for nothing and spectators from the previous bout allowed in free. One journalist suggested, perhaps with tongue in cheek, that a simpler solution would be for the fouled fighter to be allowed a free punch at his opponent's groin, while the offending boxer's hands were held behind his back.

Bryan Downie was disqualified in his world middleweight championship bout against Johnny Wilson at Cleveland in 1921. The Cleveland Boxing Commission refused to accept the verdict and awarded the title to Downie on a knockout. There was an uproar in the press and Downie was never recognised as the champion.